CANCER
BOWS TO A
Smile

Volume 2

Bruce Morton

Cancer Bows to a Smile, Volume 2

Cancer Bows to a Smile
Volume 2

Bruce Morton

Copyright © 2020

Cancer Bows to a Smile, Volume 2

Cancer Bows to a Smile, Volume 2

Contents

The Story Continues	July 15, 2019	1
Homecoming	July 23, 2019	3
Words From a Follower	July 23, 2019	5
Ya huck!	July 24, 2019	7
And So It Goes…	July 30, 2019	9
Looking Up!	July 30, 2019	11
Taking It on the Chin	August 1, 2019	13
The Obstacle Course	August 7, 2019	16
Radiation? Check!	August 12, 2019	18
Sleeping Beauty	August 13, 2019	19
A Conversation with Alexa	August 13, 2019	21
Writer's Block? Nah…	August 15, 2019	23
The Morning After	August 15, 2019	26
Tumor Humor	August 16, 2019	27
Flattened	August 21, 2019	31
Fighting Back!	August 25, 2019	32
Charm	August 27, 2019	35
Wearable Airbag for Seniors	August 26, 2019	37
Friday the 13th	August 28, 2019	39
It's Baaaack…	August 31, 2019	42
Adventures in Infusionville	September 4, 2019	43
MM, Why Did You Pick *ME?!*	September 5, 2019	44
Quanked	September 7, 2019	46
Call For Reinforcements!	September 8, 2019	49

Voices of Concern	September 13, 2019	50
Femur and Fat	September 14, 2019	51
Femur and Fat Follow-Up	September 14, 2019	53
Shots and Clots (Or Not)	October 4, 2019	57
Prayer!	October 7, 2019	60
Trials, and So Forth	October 10, 2019	61
BMB!	October 11, 2019	63
Drat! Scratch the Trial ☹	October 12, 2019	66
Keeping the Plates Spinning	October 14, 2019	67
Cherie	October 26, 2019	69
It Is Well!	October 26, 2019	72
I'm IN!	October 29, 2019	74
Therapy the Sixth	October 30, 2019	78
Thankfulness	November 9, 2019	80
Garage Therapy	November 9, 2020	83
Adventures With Gravity	November 9, 2019	86
Lowering the Lambda	November 19, 2019	89
Thanksgiving	November 28, 2019	91
Wonderfulness	November 30, 2019	93
Mole-Whacking, and So Forth	November 30, 2019	96
Clots? Lots? We're Hoping Not	December 6, 2019	98
The New Stopping Place	December 11, 2019	100
Dex Crash!	December 16, 2019	102
A Thought for Mike	December 22, 2019	105
The Best-Laid Plans…	December 26, 2019	106
The Plot Thickens	January 5, 2020	108
Go West!	January 7, 2020	111

Cancer Bows to a Smile, Volume 2

The Plot Thickens... Again	January 12, 2020	113
Meanwhile, Back at the Trial	January 12, 2020	114
Ocean Dreams	January 16, 2020	117
Flagged!	January 18, 2020	120
Happy Anniversary	January 19, 2020	122
Mike	January 20, 2020	124
Yet Another Specialist!	January 25, 2020	125
Laughter Infection	January 29, 2020	126
Side Effects	February 4, 2020	129
Again With the Side Effects	February 13, 2020	132
Spread Love!	February 13, 2020	134
Did I Mention Side Effects?	February 24, 2020	135
As They Say in "The Cape"	February 29, 2020	137
Life Is the Bubbles	March 1, 2020	139
Pain!	March 11, 2020	140
Oops... Quarantine	March 19, 2020	144
Maybe Tomorrow	March 19, 2020	145
I'm Back!	March 19, 2020	146
Goin' Home... NOT	March 20, 2020	147
FINALLY Home Again!	March 21, 2020	148
The Real Heroes	March 21, 2020	149
And Back We Go	March 25, 2020	151
Where to Go?	March 27, 2020	153
Home Again, For Now	April 3, 2020	154
"The Rest of the Story"	April 5, 2020	156
Getting Back on the Pony	April 8, 2020	162
Praying for Platelets	April 9, 2020	165

Cancer Bows to a Smile, Volume 2

Platelets and a Picture	April 10, 2020	167
Easter	April 12, 2020	169
Show Us Your Pets	April 13, 2020	170
Show Us Your Wheels	April 20, 2020	171
See, I Told You It Would Heal!	April 28, 2020	173
Changes, Maybe	April 29, 2020	175
The Way We Were	May 2, 2020	178
What About Garlic?	May 3, 2020	179
Flying Solo	May 4, 2020	180
Throwing *Out* the Towel	May 4, 2020	183
Selinexor	May 5, 2020	185
I Wanna Be Sedated	May 11, 2020	187
The Six-Month Gift	May 12, 2020	189
Sally Next Door	May 21, 2020	192
Life With Sally	May 22, 2020	193
What Did You Do Today?	June 2, 2020	194
It's the Shoulder This Time	June 14, 2020	195
Staph Meeting	June 24, 2020	198
The Rigor and the Port	June 24, 2020	201
Thoughts From a Friend	July 2, 2020	203
Bruce Juice Is Good to Go!	July 16, 2020	204
Spreading the Joy!	July 24, 2020	207
Saying No to "Sally Next Door"	July 27, 2020	209
All In Vein	July 28, 2020	213
Plotting the Course	July 31, 2020	216
The Agony of da Feet	August 1, 2020	218
Farewell To Staph!	August 5, 2020	221

Cancer Bows to a Smile, Volume 2

Pump Up the Volume (2)	August 6, 2020	223
We're Doing Number 2 ☺	August 23, 2020	226
The Road Ahead	August 23, 2020	228
Runaway Wheelchair!	August 25, 2020	232
Acknowledgments		236
Glossary and Abbreviations		240

Cancer Bows to a Smile, Volume 2

Foreword

I read over my Foreword for Volume 1 of this series, and decided to take the lazy way out and give that Foreword a hardy "'Nuff said."

However, so much happens in this Volume 2 of my journey with MM, I suppose an updated Foreword is called for.

Volume 1 was well received, so there was no need, I figured, to change the basic format in Volume 2.

What DID change was what I encounter as my MM transitions to "late stage." I'm sicker now, and (spoiler alert!) by the later postings in this volume we are down to just a few options for me: a last remaining FDA approved drug combo; a clinical trial; or waiting around for FDA approval of a CAR-T cell procedure.

When we decide on which treatment scheme we'll opt for, I'll end this Volume 2 and save my next postings for Volume 3.

I've said from the start that these books are not mine. They belong to, and are made possible, by all of us who travel our years with MM as our constant companion. I choose to accept MM as just that... my travel companion; and this book is made possible because it makes sense to "gang up" and journey together. This is OUR book... a chronicle of OUR life with MM.

Cancer Bows to a Smile, Volume 2

You have before you a series of postings and comments made to Facebook private groups that have grown up to serve those of us who have the blood cancer Multiple Myeloma.

The postings start out rather ordinary but as they continue two things start to happen. First, my journey with the disease becomes more challenging... I get sicker. And second, to better cope I decided to do a bit of mood modification by writing only uplifting postings, my mission being to stay in a positive frame of mind no matter where this cancer took me. So I posted light hearted recounts of my day with the MM.

Others in the private group found my postings funny. A relief from the daily grind of this illness.

Cancer Comedy. Tumor Humor. Strange, Huh? But all of us sorely needed to laugh more. And as we did smile and laugh more , if even for just a short while , we felt just that little bit better.

So the others encouraged me to write more. The positive comments included here may look like my attempt to glorify myself so let's be clear. It's never been about me. It's been a collective effort to bring a smile and a laugh to our lives as we travel with this cancer.

You will also learn about what it is like to travel with MM. So many challenges to health, relationships, attitude and one's faith life.

The postings have not been edited for typos. Spell checker software makes for some interesting word replacements that are left in. For privacy reasons I have removed the names of those who commented. I truly believe that a smile and a laugh is good medicine. Yes, Cancer Bows to a Smile.

Bruce Morton

brucemorton@sbcglobal.net

Editor's Note

Bruce made me write this. Honestly. I'm content to labor away behind the scenes, but he insisted I toot my horn, so… "Toot."

I first met Bruce Morton years ago at a British car show in St. Louis County. We were each showing our MG Midget sports cars, and a casual chat turned into a friendship that saw me spending many an afternoon at his house turning wrenches and trying to find electrical problems, as well as dispatching my wife's chocolate chip cookies, which are remarkable.

So I was dismayed to learn, about seven years ago, that he had contracted Multiple Myeloma. Yes, I had to look it up to see what it was. And in the years since, I've seen first-hand how this disease can change a life. No one likes to see a friend suffer, and not surprisingly I tried to help out in any way I could.

So last year, Bruce asked me if I knew anything about self-publishing, and explained that he'd received suggestions about getting some of his Facebook interactions out in book form. And lo and behold, in the past I'd helped my Dad and a friend publish a couple of books through Amazon, and was familiar with the process. One thing led to another, and *Cancer Bows to a Smile, Volume 1* was released to the world in 2019. The response was pretty exciting, and we knew that Volume 2 would have to happen eventually.

Well, happen it did, and you're holding it. Bruce is thrilled to the heart to be able to offer any encouragement he can to fellow MM sufferers, and I'm thrilled to crunch the text to make it all come together. Keep in mind that most of said text was originally generated in Facebook via Bruce's iPhone, and you get the impression that editing it all must have been a load of laughs. Yes, it was. 'Nuff said.

Most importantly, Bruce and I found out that we share a common faith in Christ, and this has made all the difference.

So enjoy Volume 2! It's been a pleasure to put it together, and we hope it brightens your day and lightens the load.

Gryf Ketcherside

The Story Continues

July 15, 2019

It's a book now. We took several of my musing and glumped them into a book. I've given out a few, and the word is it's a one-night read that's a fun read that also shows many of the challenges we encounter on our MM journey.

I came to a good stopping place on June 30. My MM is progressing and solutions that are found now are rather risky.

Kane is now my constant companion as is Oxy. I like Kane. Oxy's got to go.

Road trip with Ellie and my other friend Karen, a good friend who puts up with my kidding and nags me into behaving rightly. Ellie, Karen and me. So far the laughs have been frequent and we've only had to pull off once to laugh in the safety of a Walmart's Parking lot.

I hobble, but I don't hurt.

I'm so very thankful I'm on this trip. I'm thankful for healing in some places and we just need to wait to heal up in other places. Kane helps me get around… I'm thankful for Kane. And friend Karen makes the trip possible... thankful for her.

I'm thankful for the good breakfast I'll enjoy, and the good coffee somebody will serve me. That's such a treat for me, to get that first cup served.

Sleepy now. Catch a few winks. Take my meds, including Cipro.

And so it goes... and so it goes.

Comments:

> *I am, as always, in awe of your spirit!! It definitely does NOT have cancer. Be safe.*
>
> *Bruce, I am thrilled you printed the book. You, and your attitude, are an inspiration to many of us.*
>
> *What a beautiful title for your book.* 🙏

St. Jude Children's Research Hospital

ALSAC • Danny Thomas, Founder

Finding cures. Saving children.

Homecoming

July 23, 2019

Well, I'm back home, arriving yesterday morning around... Yawn... 2:00 a.m... After a long, long 16 hour drive.

We are "tarred" (which in Cape Girardeau speak is like 'tuckered' only more, much more...) and Karen goes right to bed.

Karen likes not to be confused with my sister, Karen... This Karen is my "friend with benefits" Karen.

(That's right, and a perfect "friend with benefits" she is. Psssst. Hey fellas listen up. I'm saying it. The benefits you long for, yep. My "friend with benefits..." yeah.

She owns an RV!!!

Karen lives 'bout two hours from here and she cares for me when we go on a trip. (Which I didn't... I didn't trip, I mean but came close... but that was Kane's fault every time.) Oh, and my other traveling partner Mr. Oxy helped along the way.

Here's a Googled nugget of knowledge I'll pack in the back of my chemo brain: A lesion on the femur bone can be bad. Can hurt. Can significantly weaken the entire bone and that means it breaks and that can hurt like a whole bunch more, bad.

My MM specialist (you all have one, right? If you don't go to a MM specialist for your care... well, uh... well... well, you should) gave me the okay to go on my annual trip to Colorado if I promised to be careful on that femur;" NO MOUNTAIN BIKING FOR YOU!!!!"

Yeah, yeah... a femur bone with a honkin' large lesion... a genuine Rocky Mountain trail with honkin' large rocks... a mountain bike in the weakened hands of a tourist with his pesky tumors... What could go wrong?

Back to the ol' grind now though. Echocardiogram with contrast today. Tomorrow, labs, appt with the doc, pitch some woo at that first receptionist. Kyprolis infusion. Wednesday, Kyprolis infusion. Thursday, appt with the orthopedic surgeon (Can you say "surgery"???) Friday, sit and wait for FedEx to deliver my first cycle of Pomalyst.

Yep, having MM is a full time job.

And so it goes, and so it goes.

Words From a Follower

July 23, 2019

One of my "flock" on Facebook wrote this about me on her Facebook page to tell her friends about me.

Her description of me now is quite accurate!

Enjoy...

> Ala Bruce Morton:
>
> Bruce wrote a book called Cancer Bows To A Smile which I have - it's hysterical - you can get it on Amazon.
>
> Bruce has started his second book.
>
> Bruce has Multiple Myeloma - like me.
>
> Bruce believes he is late stage and has dedicated his life now to medical trials, writing, and his MG sports car, but I believe God has purpose for him, so he has a ways to go.
>
> Bruce lives alone with his dog Ellie and no longer has a caretaker.
>
> Bruce sleeps in his recliner in his "almost living" living room.
>
> Bruce has learned to give himself his own IVs at home.

Bruce is Covid free.

Bruce is an amazing inspiration to me and many others with MM.

Bruce reminds me that small adventures make a life, do what can be done, and trust heavily on the Lord... Be grateful..... Smile!

Because cancer can't beat a smile.

And remember, someone else needs more than you do no matter how bad you've got it.

Almost every day Bruce makes me laugh, not just smile.

His story should be heard by more than just MM patients.

Let SparkCures find a Multiple Myeloma trial for you!
SparkCures.com | 888-828-2206

Ya huck!

July 24, 2019

Well, my friend Karen went back home today after our week in Colorado. She lives in "Mid Missouri" on a small farm 'bout two hours from here near a trout steam where we fish together when I'm healthy, alas.

I saw the doc today with sister Karen. The doc has a different patient on his hands here of late.

We are playing "Whack-a-Mole" with my MM.

Over here we whack at a tumor on my back and over there appears a lesion on my femur... whack... oops... a miss... only to reveal a new lesion on my sternum... whack... a miss... but oh, so close!

Trying a new treatment scheme of Kyprolis and Pomalyst... whack, whack... wait for it...

The doc is the expert, and he's the "warrior" doing the whacking. He hits the mark. Yeah, I have a great warrior doc.

My job is to be the healing guy and make people smile.

We laughed out loud together at my appointments, though the news of my condition provided little to make light of.

Now, oops, the kidneys are beginning to act up. Shhhh, settle back now, kidneys. "Whack!!!!" Ha!

Taking Kyprolis that has a history of whacking my heart. The doc applies the perfect dose to safely whack back at the MM. And we wait for lab results.

Ha! Whack! Will that first dose of Kyprolis hit the mark? Ha? Second dose is later this morning. Whack!

We will land a big smile on this day. This glorious day in MM-ville.

Ha! Whack! Smile.

And so it goes and so it goes!

Comments:

> Keep smiling and keep US smiling! You're the best.

> Yes. Kyprolis is tough. I am on a break from it right now because it was making me so sick I had to have a blood transfusion. But... I will be back on in mid-August. "And so it goes...

> What on Earth does "ya huck" mean? [Goofy the Disney character.]

And So It Goes...
July 30, 2019

Oh my, oh my, this MM has temporarily got position on me and is running the show.

Ha! But it's not for long.

One by one, me and the doc will push back on the MM at each point.

Right now the tumor on my right femur is troubling, but we will soon blast that with radiation.

And I'm being told to give up Kane and stick to a walker.

Today I get dosed with Kyprolis and Pomalyst.

The Pom is making me so tired. *So* tired. Yesterday I was horizontal the entire day.

This combo of Krypolis and Pom needs to work, as my MM is clearly out of the box and the PET scan I recently had showed lots of lesions. Yikes!

I'm seeing lots of specialists... the ortho surgeon for my leg really knows her stuff. And my radiologist is top-notch.

Ten radiation treatments and several more cycles of the combo treatment are in my future before I can turn this thing around.

I'll try to post about my journey but some days I'm just a blank.

Thanks to everyone for wondering about me!

Comments:

Hang in there!!

Bruce, I am sending hugs and prayers. My biggest prayer is for God's healing hands to touch and heal your body mind and spirit! I also hope that there will be laughter for you again soon. Rest my friend and take care of yourself.

Never give up the fight! In our hearts we are with you every step of the way. Hope your treatment goes well. Take all the rest you need — we'll be here waiting for your wonderful words.

Hang in there... God is stronger than the cancer!

Looking Up!

July 30, 2019

Ah ha! And thanks to your-alls' prayers and best wishes... I'll pause whilst (whilst is UK speak for "while") you do a much deserved collective pat on the back, yeah.

I walkered in to the Cancer Center where my blood labs for today showed improvement in four - count 'em, FOUR - areas! My whites are up. My platelets are up. And my hemoglobin is up. AND my kidney creatine which had decided to spike for no reason has now fallen and is headed toward being "in range" Yip Yip Yippee!

I got home and Ellie said "See I told you you'd be fine."

Next up is to see my important Lambda Light Chain number fall fall fall whilst (now what did we learn about whilst???) my heart keeps on a pumping.

(See, it was opined that last time I was dosed with Kyprolis that it whacked my heart and sent ole Bruce a gaspin' for his next breath to the first responders. The doc quickly decided "No more Kyprolis for YOU!"... and he flatly refused to give me Kyprolis again, even though a cardiologist said my heart is fine, and that it wasn't the Kyprolis that sent me to the ER. Once my MM rocketed to a high point and other treatment possibilities dried up, Kyprolis combined with Pomalyst and Dex is what we are betting on...which is fine with me).

So we count our blessings.

We are thankful this glorious day!

In just ONE DAY we get improvement in FOUR important areas.

Whack! Ha!

And so it goes. And so it goes.

Comments:

Great news, Bruce! Celebrating with you.

That's really great news! And I, too, love reading your posts and hearing how upbeat you are even whilst in the midst of some pretty nasty stuff!

KPd has been working for me for over 3 years.

Woohooooo!!! Hip, hip, hooray!

Taking It On The Chin

August 1, 2019

It began so innocently.

At the Cancer Center infusion lounge I picked a chair near the window.

In the goodies basket there was a special treat that would soon cause a mini chaos throughout the entire lounge. And yours truly is involved, so the tale needs a tellin'.

Once I'm hooked to the drip, drip, drip of Kyprolis and settled in is when things go sour.

A nice fellow seats himself and his caregiver right next to me and at that point the caregiver announces himself with authority: a snotty cough.

Ugh, this might change things.

So I mask up. Of course.

But I mostly wants that new treat in the goodie basket: Famous Amos Mini Chocolate Chip Cookies!!! I snag a bag. Ha!

But remember, I'm still masked up.

So without removing my mask I decide to slide each FACCC between the mask and my fully grayed out beard smooshing the chocolate chips hard against the light background of my beard on the way to my mouth... leaving, unbeknownst to me, chocolate chip skid marks all up my chin.

I'm a total mess at half bag but I continue on to finish the entire bag.

Take just a moment to picture what I look like with all those FACCC chocolate chips ground into my chin!

Before long my caregiver sister, Karen, looks up from her current issue of "Magnolia" to check on me. She sees and sorta doesn't see that sumfin is not right 'bout Bruce's chin.

"What's that on your chin???!!!"

Unlike some others, I guess, I can't look down and see my chin. Try it... right now look down at your chin.

So I'm at a loss for what I can do to find what might be on my chin. I look down... TWICE!!! I rub my chin with my free hand (as the steady drip, drip of K continues into my right hand) and I remember saying "chocolate chip cookies" as my answer to "What's that on your chin???" But by then sweet Karen is rushing off to get a wetted paper towel...

"SO YOUNG MAN WHAT IS THAT MESS ON YOUR CHIN!!!" She scrubs whilst holding me still like I'm eight years old. You moms know that vise-like grab, and it *hurts*.

Nothing rubs off so that means my scrub down has attracted the attention of the nurses. And THAT attracts the attention of the entire lounge of cancer patients gettin' infused.

The second nurse on the scene rubbed a goo of some sort that smelled mediciney and since whatever it was on my chin weren't there no more I was declared ok and everybody just left.

Karen was soon back to her "Magnolia" issue.

Me? I was back to the drip, drip, drip...

And so it goes, and so it goes.

Comments:

> *I often entertained myself while getting an infusion....once the nurses were concerned about a man's port. He quietly informed them he had spilled CHOCOLATE MILKSHAKE all over it.*
>
> *Oh my, Bruce Morton, a rough morning & then your post became my next center of attention. God Bless you for all your upbeat fun you spread today.*
>
> *Good for you on grabbing your bag of cookies.* 😊 😊 *You tell your stories in a real cute way! You always make me laugh...*

The Obstacle Course
August 7, 2019

Ok... little halp for the newly hobbled one.

It appears as if my BFF might just be Kane (I.e., I'll be walking with a cane so as to not put full weight on my tumor-weakened left leg.) Darn it anyway. But it don't pain me none. (Which is Cape Girardeau speak for "it does not hurt," which is good.)

So I've made some changes, but I could use a few more suggestions for gettin' around safely at home. Give me some tips, please.

(Speaking of "tips" I learned there are special, more pliable "cane" tips that give better traction than rubber chair tips... Who knew?)

So now the three canes I have scattered around the house have fresh tips. I tell ya, I am one happy clomper.)

Since it's a no-no for me to trek to the basement... (doc says if I stumble I'll crack my femur in half... major ouch town... first responders, the whole 911 routine) we set up the washer/dryer on the first floor. I had my "guy" (my "guy" is for a for-hire home repairman and he's a good one. We share a common language and he's even more "country" than me, dag-nabbit.) put a small combo washer dryer into what was previously the main hall coat closet. So no more need to go to the basement and risk halving my femur.

Oh oh - AND I had him install a "dog door" for Ellie. So now on the days when I'm horizontal all the live long day, Ellie lets herself in and out.

AND he put in a "Smart" Wi-Fi thermostat so I can adjust the house temp on my iPhone right from my recliner in my "barely living" room. Oh boy!

So halp me out. What other changes can I make to get this place more livable? (And don't say, "Vacuum" because I hate vacuuming and it scares Ellie, too.)

And so it goes and so it goes.

Comments:

> *Think about putting some grab bars in the bathroom and look for tripping hazards where carpet meets wood or tile?*

> *Get an Alexa and the smart light bulbs so you can turn lights on and off with voice control. They are expensive but safety first... oh and my mom is loving your book!* 😁

> *Just joined. Love this banter! Will check your book out Bruce Morton.*

Radiation? Check!

August 12, 2019

Whelp, radiation treatment #1 is ova.

They "mapped" me again and this time the Sharpie marked out a much bigger area than when I had that "who-ha" on my L3. This time Area 51 is about the size of a taco; the who-ha on the back was about half that size. So this ain't no "who-ha," it's a genuine "whoa-diggy," and the zapping took about twice as long also.

The smiley face I'd drawn on my leg was a big hit, as were my new commemorative red shoes.

Comments:

Whoa Diggity!!! Did you say Tacos!! And rock those Red Crocs!

Love the shoes!

That is a bigger area! Keep on smiling and making people around you feel your joy! The pain you feel isn't always HOW you feel. Keep shining Bruce! Love the Crocs! 😁

Loving the red power shoes. And who ding doggie on the larger areas ☺ hoping you're all through & resting back at home. 🙏🙏🙏 💖

Sleeping Beauty

August 13, 2019

Boy howdy, did I ever sleep today!

First stop in the morning was the Cancer Center for the first of ten radiation treatments to the whoa-diggy on my femur.

This time through the ray machine it seem to me to go longer than my last visit for radiation for the two who-ha's on my back.

And this time, oncet I got home, I was da-da-done for... plopped in da bed and did not get up until 6 p.m.!

I knew I was alive because I could still blink. Ellie dog sat vigil in the bedroom with me though she could have gone outside. She would nudge me awake from time to time just to be certain I'd not died without having fed her.

So, fellow MM travelers, does a massive dose of x-rays strafed into the femur make a person assume the horizontal position for an entire day. Geez... I've got nine more treatments yet to go. I'll have to change my jammies like three more times!

But tomorrow I've made the commitment to get up and move.

It's "Bruce On the Loose" day!!!

The plan is to put on my new red Crocs... get Kane in one hand and Ellie in the other and walk the neighborhood and be pointed at.

They (the neighbors) probably haven't seen me in this hobbled state and I *know* they haven't seen my red shoes. There's a reasonable chance somebody will offer up some sweets... "I'll bring you snickerdoodles later" and it's just a good thing to do a "how's his cancer" lap around the cul-de-sacs.

I hope to make it to the end of the driveway before noon, by golly.

And so it goes. And so it goes...

Comments:

Yes! Get up and get moving tomorrow. Even if it is to the front door and then to the not-so-living room! 😄

A Conversation with Alexa
August 13, 2019

Bruce: Alexa... Temperature.

Alexa: Right now it's 86 degrees Fahrenheit. Expect a low of 69 degrees.

Bruce: Alexa... Not the outdoor temperature, *my* temperature. I might have a fever.

Alexa: Ok, I'll play songs from *Saturday Night Fever*... "Well you can tell by the way I do my walk..."

Bruce: Alexa... no no no! SHUT DOWN!

Alexa: Why don't you go change into fresh jammies? You are ripe!

Bruce: Alexa... Leave me alone, or I'll slur my words and confuse you.

Bruce: Alexa... Where's my junk?

Alexa: You mean, "Where's my stuff?" you know very well where your junk is. That's not funny anymore, Morgan.

Bruce: Alexa... it's Morton, not Morgan! Ok ok, "where's my stuff?"

Alexa: Your Three Wheel walker in Pale Blue is just nine steps away.

Bruce: Alexa... I just took 20mg of Dexamethasone.

Alexa: `Oh foo, I HATE Dex days. Do you plan on yelling at me? Threatening to toss me against a wall?`

Bruce: Alexa... yeah I just might if you smart off to me like on most Dex days!

Alexa: `I do not.`

Bruce: Alexa... you hockey puck! You know you do. Last time you wouldn't stop calling me "Morgan" and playing *Best of Debbie Boone* and making fart noises when I have visitors!

Alexa: `It makes everyone smile... That's the idea, right?`

Bruce: Alexa... I'm in charge of the smiles around here, and you need to stop annoying me.

Alexa: `So you are annoyed. That's not my fault.`

Bruce: Alexa... No it's the fault of the Dex. But you join in every time!

Alexa: `Grow up.`

Bruce: Alexa... Shut up!

Alexa???

ALEXA!!!!

Writer's Block? Nah...

August 15, 2019

No "writer's block" resides here!

I'll only get thru a chunk now. The rest of the story is in the running for an "Over The Top Stress" trophy.

I'll get to that part in a 2nd post.

Two days in a row Dex was on Morgan's Medicine Menu.

Not a wink of sleep overnight. (See where this is going?)

Now I know some of us use that "up all night" time to do laundry, or vacuum.

Well in the drawer of my night stand I found a front badge from an MG sports car...(I have two restored MGs in my garage that I can't part with but also can't contort myself sufficient to get out of once gravity alone did all the "get in" work.)

So I mounted that badge on the front of my newly Amazoned three wheel walker for here at home.

I also mounted a ding-ding bell. And a bicycle speedometer/odometer. A bicycle headlight is on the way... it's an LED good for 100,000 hours of use which is remarkably reassuring.

Survey Time!!!

So folks, should I pop for one dem squeeze bulb horns?

It's 6:30am now. First light. There's a doe deer that's nursing two fawns. Every morning somewhere in the neighborhood if you are up early which, technically I was... sorta... Two fawns nursing, the mom deer on the lookout. A glorious day already, methinks!

The Dex taken at 4am kicks in.

Here in the Midwest... (to some it's called "Little Dixie" like "Cape" where I'm from...) there's this really LOUD bug called a cicada. This time of year is lovemaking time for the cicada... yack and buzz. VERY LOUD!

I only mention the cicadas because when I'm on Dex the yack and buzz is already in my head. WHOA! I truly can't distinguish the cicadas from the Dex buzz!

And so our hero leaps boldly into the day! No sleep and dosed on D.

First call is to Washington University Physicians billing department. They left a "call us" message yesterday. I... ahem... may have gotten a bit "behind." (Lemme see... TWO hospital stays... two

CT scans... two MRI scans... a PET scan... a spinal tap test and work up... Lots of X-ray imaging...

Ten radiation treatments to my L3... ortho specialist... radiology specialist...)

They want $385... and NOW BUSTER .

Nothing a little light arguing and Dex assisted enthusiasm can't resolve, eh?

(He dials and they pick up... my behind has grown... $425 now.)

And so it goes and so it goes.

STAY TUNED !!

My next stop was radiation treatment #3...

Then the 6th call to City of St. Louis Parking violation department ...we are let's just say "at a serious impasse" (hmmmm, in Cape Girardeau we drop the "e")

Then I get stood up for a lunch date... on Dex it don't take much to set off a landslide of emotion...

I don't know when I'll post but it's a couple of tales that need tellin'.

And so it goes and so it goes.

The Morning After
August 15, 2019

I've decided my day with our old friend Mr. Dex stories from yesterday need not be retold here.

Simply put, I was bludgeoned by events beyond my influence... fully dosed on Dex, following two sleepless nights. It wasn't pretty.

We all know what that's like.

And when I stumble into that kind of chaos I can leave behind quite a mess. Or smear a heaping helping of mess on myself.

(He sighs...)

So I find a steak in the freezer... a Bud Light longneck, 7oz size.

Click, click - I help the kids at St. Jude Children's Research Hospital, my fav charity.

I shower. Fresh jammies. Walker into the barely living living room. Ellie comes over to do those things dogs do to help carry us through.

Dose with evening meds that will include some "breakthrough" oxy.

I felt better in no time.

And so it goes, and so it goes.

Tumor Humor

August 16, 2019

"The tumor. How big is it? No one has ever said."

So the "doc for the day" who'd just finished glancing at my all-important tumor guest book (i.e. my radiology chart) politely offers back:

"Here, Mr. Morgan...I'll just show you."

BTW it's currently running about 50/50 as to new docs or nurses getting my name right... I answer to either Morton or Morgan... ("Norton" though for some reason I don't like and that produces a labored sigh and a kind correction "It's 'Morton' with an 'M'")

He shows me an X-ray on the PC.

I say: "That looks like a spine. "

He says: "Yes."

I say: "I'm here today for radiation treatment on my left femur."

He says: "Oh... yes, of course Mr. Morgan. My bad."

(I'm GUSHING with confidence in this fellow at this point.)

Click... click... click... click... click... click...

Almost there... click... click... click.

He says: "Date of birth?"

I tell him...

"Ok Mr. Morton...let's take a look."

(Hmmmm this guy is polite AND he now has my name right ... I'm suddenly very encouraged about him.)

This time the pic is of a femur, not a spine... my name is spelled correctly on the top bar of the screen AND that's my DOB!

Land of Goshen!!! ("Land of Goshen" is Cape Girardeau speak... it's like a big gasp... one hand on the cheek, jaw drops, to express total surprise.)

"Hey isn't that MY femur? "

And it IS!!

☺

He points...

"See here... this darker area... that is the tumor we are treating today."

I thought there would be a bulge, but no. Just a darker-toned area.

He tells me that the tumor has damaged... weakened... the femur bone in and around that area.

Now the conversation gets peppered with food analogies (get it... PEPPERED with food analogies... I made that up!!)

"So how big is it?"

"About the size of... size of...."

I jump in to help him...

"A wedge of an orange?"

"Noooo... it's bigger than that."

"A whole wheat bread toast point?" I triangulate my two hands.

Yes!

"That there is the damaged area... it's now... it's now ... got little holes in it."

"Like Swiss cheese?"

"No smaller holes"

"Baby Swiss?"

"Smaller."

(I had no food come to mind that has smaller holes than Baby Swiss cheese... dang Chemo brain... so I just go with "small holes.")

"It's weak and could crumble."

"Like a piece of Melba toast?"

"No... not THAT weak... just 'weaker.' There's no way to know how weak, though."

So my "look see" at the tumor did little to help me decide yay or nay on femur surgery as my next adventure in MM-land.

It's shaped and about the size of a whole wheat bread toast point perforated and weakened with lots of holes that are smaller than the holes in Baby Swiss cheese. The area is not as crumbly as Melba toast, certainly, and they really can't tell me how much risk for breakage there is.

Five more treatments next week.

And so it goes and so it goes.

Comments:

> Bruce oh Bruce...what are we gonna do with you? 🙊👍☺ You need that Dr./Scientist from Jurassic Park that recreated the dinosaurs out of fossils and frogs' DNA!!! 😁 #DOUSINGTHEFLAMESONMULTIPLEMYELOMA

Flattened

August 21, 2019

I'm off my usual posting to Facebook schedule.

Fatigue from the radiation and dual immunotherapy drugs has me laid out and dehydrated, I think.

Help is on the way to get me to some hydration bags and my Kyprolis infusion at noon.

I'll be fine.

Do Da Do Da Do Da
Doot Da Doot Da Doot Da Da

That's the bugle call of the cavalry from the ole cowboy movie... Wagons are circling, Native American savages are being run off.

And all is well ... I'll post an update later.

And so it goes and so it goes.

Comments:

Praying for you Bruce. I just got your book and I love it!

Prayers for you Bruce!

Fighting Back!

August 25, 2019

Every so often my MM gets the upper hand.

And as my disease progresses, there's more to deal with than in the early years of this.

But that's ok.

MM gets its shot at me. We deal with it all and do what we can to get position on the MM... and get back to a somewhat more normal "new normal."

Just now, and for the last several weeks, MM is being quite a bother.

Slowly though we are starting to turn things around.

Yay!

Not to drag everyone through my journey, but here's the skinny; My treatment scheme is Kyprolis and Pomalyst plus the tumor. It's a rather big one, by golly... the tumor on my femur is getting zapped with radiation treatment rays. Oh boy!

That triple whammy lays me out flat... fatigue... the "F word!!"

I regularly sleep 16-18 hours at a stretch which is how I spent my Sunday. So, when I awake I'm seriously dehydrated and I know it.

Bring on the Gatorade and the breakthrough oxy for the pain from tumor.

Get myself fed. Consider calling a friend to come put a rescue effort to me but I start to feel better so I don't... save that for another time.

The KPD treatment isn't working... my important Lambda Light Chain marker jacked up 50% last week... Yikes!

Port surgery on Tuesday... my veins have collapsed and an "arm draw" just doesn't cut it any more.

I see the ortho surgeon on Tuesday to schedule them putting a rod in to support my weakened femur.

But NONE of that is important. The docs will handle all that just fine.

What's important is that I get around okay on one good leg until the other one heals.

I made changes here at home, because chances are I'll be hobbled for quite a long while. We moved the washer/dryer up from the basement.

I bot me one dem Roomba vacs because trying to vacuum with Kane was just ridiculous... think about that sight. The vac is named Vic, and he does a fine job... mops the kitchen floor, too.

This coming week we turn the tables in MM and we are so looking forward to that. Ha!

My friend will be here on Thursday to rescue me. Bring me some special brownies. Clean the place before the board of health hears how I've been living.

With this disease we must expect the mmmmmm... (setbacks, which is a word I don't use). We are stronger and smarter than our MM. Our docs have seen it all and they know just what to do.

Step aside, MM.

And so it goes and so it goes

Comments:

> *Hang in there, Brother. There is always another option!*
>
> *Hang in there Bruce. I love reading your posts. Beat the heck out of that MM.*
>
> *Thanks for sharing the journey. It's not all wine and roses. I admire your sense of humor.*

Charm

August 27, 2019

Hee hee. Yesterday I was only awake for a short while. (I've been doin' the deep snooze thing most days... fatigue from radiation and treatment).

Posted some thoughts on Facebook, but I was so groggy it was a rather lame effort.

I returned a few Messenger contacts. Again, lame effort; I was half asleep, and the other half was dozing.

(I really like Messenger on Facebook; it's a good way to reach out to me.)

Made a couple of phone calls; one call was to a lady that made quite an impression on me.

She was utterly and thoroughly... well, she was...

Charming.

Yep, charming, she was.

And I think that's just marvelous; to journey with this cancer and yet retain our charm.

So today at my last radiation zap to my femur tumor (note to self... I need to name my femur tumor... something snappy to reflect my love and affection) I said something to the Tech.

I simply said... "I like you."

That's hardly a charming statement, but it made her day.

We can do that, all through our meet ups with others.

Make 'em smile and make 'em feel good about themselves.

Thanks, charmer from yesterday... I feel better because I've met you!

Charm.

And so it goes and so it goes.

Comments:

Today is my crash day from Dex. Just can't wake up. Forcing myself up as I have things that should be done today Trying to be responsible.

You needed yr rest dear ...my husband takes his naps but never can get a good long night of sleep...I think it's the steroids... you're a champ.

You are truly an inspiration, in every regard. Thanks Bruce! ♥

Wearable Airbag for Seniors

August 26, 2019

What, huh???

(Google it. Now... you know you want to.)

It's just as it's named. It's made for seniors because they figure seniors fall oftener than non-seniors.

And sure as shine it *is* an AIRBAG like what's in your car.

Yep and the idea is for Pa Pa (or Me Ma) to strap this airbag around their middle... it's got "tip over" sensors in it so it knows when the fall starts;

Then Kablooey... it inflates in an instant, and all injury is avoided.

I first heard about a WAFS about a half year ago when mom (she's 93) kept falling. A broken hip at her age would be bad.

Mom weighs in at about 110 pounds so a wearable airbag exploding on her might make it hard to find her afterwards.

"Where's Mom?"

So we nixed that idea for mom. But now the WAFS is for me.

I've got this pig of a tumor on my femur, and if I take a hard fall the femur will become "femurs," which is bad and hurts and I'll scream like a monkey...

But the WAFS will cushion me. Injury avoided.

I'll see the ortho surgeon tomorrow and see what she says. Maybe she will write me a script for a WAFS....

(I am gonna ask the doc. Ha! This should be fun...,)

And so it goes and so it goes.

Comments:

> *I love humor, but you know how to take something so painful and difficult and make me laugh. I had another cancer 22 years ago when I was young, and I used humor all the time, and I watched funny movies, and it helped so much. I call MM the Whack-a-Mole disease. My doctor and nurses love the name. I used to be an oncology nurse, and now I teach. Something is always popping up somewhere, just like the Whack-a-Mole game.*
>
> *Wahahaha this one got my funny bone! And I don't find much funny these days!* ♥ 😁 😊 ♥

Friday the 13th
August 28, 2019

Friday the 13th of September... prophylactic intramedullary nail, left femur.

Yep surgery is all scheduled.

The doc would not go for the wearable airbag scheme, and instead made me agree to unfriending Kane and going with the walker at all times until the 13th. Drat!

Calling it a "nail" is unsettling but I'm told the procedure is a rather simple one which is good to know... I suppose... seeing as how it involves a nail and general anesthesia.

Don't overthink this one, Morton.

So what's the big deal, eh?

On Friday the 13th, a hole is made in your pelvis and a nail is slipped into the bone cavity of the femur displacing bone marrow into the leg muscle... two screws tie the nail to good bone at the bottom, and two at the upper end. And...

Bob's your uncle... all done. (Google "Bobs your uncle" if you don't already know what that's all about. Our MM travelers in the UK know all about Bob's Uncle.)

So, tonight -

Don't overthink it... dose a couple of Oxy for the pain... Yippee. Feeling fine in no time!

Oh and -

Today I got my "power" port put in.

What means this "power" he asks? I'm told the new design of this bad boy means it can handle a bigger squirt (oxymoron? you decide) of whatever they want to inject into me. Comes in handy with the first responders in the ambulance, I'm told, and it was ordered special just for me. Gulp!

Don't overthink it, Morton.

So we arrived at the Cancer Center at 8 a.m. and pulled out onto Euclid Ave at 4:30 p.m. LONG day, BUT we got free parking... I snagged two dem little snickers bites and AND a bag of Famous Amos mini choc chip cookies... AND I gave a copy of our book to my friend and former employer Rodger Riney; I enjoyed doing that.**

Sister Karen, my caregiver, worked a double shift today. Thanks, sister. (She will be relieved by friend with benefits Karen tomorrow.)

And so it goes and so it goes.

**Yes the name Rodger Riney may be familiar to you. Rodger is a fellow MM traveler. He and I are being treated by the same doc. Recently Rodger and his wife Paula donated $22 million for MM research at Washington University School of Medicine. Their generosity will benefit each and every one of us. Eh.

And so it goes and so it goes,

Comments:

> *Had this procedure done three years ago! No more pain since!*
>
> *Love the power port. I have had mine for about 8 months. Doesn't hurt much to access.*
>
> *I got nailed! No problems. After the cut heals and they remove the staples, you will forget it's there until you try to go through the fast line at the airport.*
>
> *That's a good date! You'll feel so much better afterwards, it's a different kind of pain but I was up walking on it the next morning. Granted I broke two of my titanium rods six months later and had to have a replacement, but that's how I roll. Can I screw it up, yes I can!*

It's Baaaack…

August 31, 2019

Well, well, well.

It's baaaaaaack.

That pesky tumor on my sternum is back and all poochy-outtie.

The PET scan from a month ago showed show there might be some MM activity on my sternum.

Now it's a thang, so bring on the radiation.

Fiddlesticks!

Bruce Hornsby said it best; "That's just the way it is…"

And so it goes and so it goes.

Comments:

Damn, sternum tumors are the worst. 😕 *No sneezing. When one comes up, pinch your nose as hard as you can. Did they already radiate that spot? I am not sure there are repeats in the same area. Get yourself in a CAR-T trial ASAP.* 🙆😳❤

So sorry to hear. Freaking Myeloma is just a sneaky, nasty disease. Hope the radiation zaps that tumor right outta there!

Adventures in Infusionville

September 4, 2019

Whilst getting me ready for the 10 minute squirt of Kyprolis, I mentioned to the nurse that my newly installed port hurt when they did the blood draw at the previous station.

She informed that there was a prescription Lanacane cream available to help soothe the area. Schmoosh some on an hour before infusion, and ta-da, no pain.

Just then a nice caregiver fellow leaned in from around the curtain and opined that his wife swears by the stuff. One cancer traveler helping another! His wife was there laid out... getting her infusion... leukemia....

So I gave him a copy of our book, *Cancer Bows to a Smile*. We gave him and her a smile, I'll betcha!

Our book. Give away a copy and bring a smile where it's needed.

Headed back to get more Kyprolis today.

And so it goes and so it goes.

MM, Why Did You Pick *Me*?!
September 5, 2019

WhoaKay, it's 2am... and I'm juiced on Dex just waitin' for sunrise and my cheap store brand corn flakes breakfast and at 7a I'll go to get briefed on the safety (or not) of general anesthesia. "It's completely safe Mr. Morgan, we never make ANY mistakes! (?)"

An age-old question I ponder these wee hours of the morning in MM-ville: "What might I have encountered in overabundance in my life that made me a select target for MM?"

Four possa bill ah teez:

Radon gas... I've live here for 42 years; so I did a test, and this place tested WAY out of range.

Epoxy automobile paint. VERY dangerous stuff. I restored a bunch of British sports cars... What Ho! And them fumes was baaaad.

Lead soldiers... I had and played with brigades and brigades of *real* lead soldiers as a kid. (And people wondered at the time "Is he 'right'"??) I got over that. Or did I ? Hmmmmmm.

And lastly ... and this one is THE one. This is the one that did me in! And, sadly, my own mother is to blame. She SLATHERED me in the stuff. DAILY!!! And the SMELL... To this day, just thinking about the smell sickens me. Others may not be wise to this. For you, alas, you heard it here first:

Campho Phenique!

And so it goes and so it goes.

Comments:

> *My oncologist suggested not even think about "why" I got Myeloma. He felt you're just going to make yourself "crazy" trying to figure it out, & you'll never really know the reason.*
>
> *Bruce Morton, the things that go through the mind of a MM warrior. Why, how and what??? We will never know. Just know that we were chosen to deliver this message whether we like it or not. Learning how to live an altered life. Bruce I often wonder too, but cannot think of an answer. Never exposed to the things you mentioned (at least to that level). ☺ We WILL beat this!!*

Let SparkCures find a Multiple Myeloma trial for you!
SparkCures.com | 888-828-2206

Quanked

September 7, 2019

What's to be done to manage the "F" word side effect: Fatigue?

Quanked. The "Q" word of MM.

I've been thoroughly quanked for days in a row during the "rest" times of treatment. Week after week. Quanked.

But I found a fatigue solution! And it works! Yep and by golly.

I've employed this method successfully to get at my own fatigue and I'm here to reveal the secret three part solution.

(I'll veer off course here for just a sec and comment on the much-published fatigue solution that I never found to be plausible for me. The idea is to exercise your way through the tiredness. Huh? What? I'll ask you others out there in MM-ville, can exercise help with fatigue?)

Ok, Morgan's Fatigue Solution! Three everyday, 'round the house items.

First... one small... I said ONE, and I said SMALL... brownie. My 'friend with benefits' makes 'em up for me.

Second... one, straight from the fridge raspberry yogurt. Has to be raspberry. No substitutions.

Third... 12-17 hours of mostly continuous bedrest and deep sleep interrupted only for urination.

Stay in bed. No driving!

DO NOT INCREASE first or second part. Add only to the third part: more sleep.

And there you have it. Ta Da!

Your body will tell you what you need. Listen to your body. (I can't stand that "listen to your body" rubbish. My body makes gross, ugly noises and I've no desire to listen. Ever. And you can't make me. So there.)

Ok, back to the Morgan three part Fatigue Solution. Works for me.

And so it goes and so it goes.

So, what's your fav fatigue solution? Tell us!

Comments:

> *It's okay to sleep away... your body needs rest!!! I on the other hand can't sleep at all, even though I'm tired. One dilemma or the other?? Still praying* ☺☺

> *I nap most days, sometimes with an Ativan. No brownies available.*

I haven't come up with my favorite solution yet... I'm usually too tired to think about a solution, so bed it is. Just received my Medical marijuana card so hoping once I have my consultation, we will come up with a daytime and nighttime solution. I'm not looking for the same energy I had a couple of years ago, I know that's not possible, but enough to get me through a day without desperately wanting/needing a nap. We'll see.

Thank you so much for sharing that exercise IS a valid and valuable solution for fatigue. I agree. It's not for everyone though, and that's what's good about the ideas we share here. We can try what works for others; they might be a solution for ourselves.

My local onc prescribed Ritalin (ADHD drug) off-label for its energy side effect; the generic, Methylphenidate 20mg morning and noon, 20mgs in 2017 (?). I pay for it since not covered as prescribed off-label. It quit working recently and I believe I have developed a tolerance for it. Also you can try Modafinil, a work shift Rx treatment.

When I feel quanked, I drink espresso and push through it... walk my dog for a few miles etc. No matter how quanked I am... I'm up by 6 am... if I ever nap, something is seriously wrong... despite the beast!!

Call For Reinforcements!

September 8, 2019

Here's looking at the rod soon to be ever so gently crammed inside my femur and ratchet screwed to my remaining "good" bone at the ends. (Sound effects: NASCAR pit stop!!!)

Procedure takes place on Friday, and they say I'll be out of the hospital next day; to which I said "BOULDERDASH!!!" You people will keep me 'til Monday, sure as shootin'.

And so it goes and so it goes.

Comments:

> *Wow! Praying for you my friend. We need you up and walking so we can go out on the town next month!!!* 😀 💪 🙏

Voices of Concern

September 13, 2019

Is something going on with Bruce Morton? I've seen some worrying posts.

He is having a rod put in his femur today.

Prayers for Bruce Morton today and a speedy recover. My mom has a rod in her femur and it was a definite improvement. May God give you the same result... and so it goes.

We are with you in spirit Bruce. Love ya!!

Bruce Morton - your family of warriors are pulling for you.

Femur and Fat

September 14, 2019

Whelp, here's the Reader Digest version of "where's Bruce?" (Thanks to all who've asked about me and sent along best wishes.)

Yesterday was Friday the 13th *and* a full Harvest Moon. Spooky!

So I brought along my Jason mask and red hat along with me to the hospital.

Uh oh. The hospital! What is it?

(It's a huge building with lots of sick people, but that's not important right now.)

What *is* important is that Bruce was in the hospital to have a support rod installed in his left femur to repair damage done by a tumor.

And the operation went fabulous... just GREAT! In fact, today they had me up and walking in my walker. Very little pain.

But remember, this is Bruce we are talking about here; and I am the king of making a simple hospital procedure much more complicated than need be.

But, learned a new hospital term: **Fat Embolism**.

Ok, see, the simple operation is to slide a rod inside the femur.

But that displaces what's in the femur... in rare cases, to the blood stream. My femur had some fat cells in it; next thing you know, those fat cells travelled to my lungs and heart. Not good.

That sent the operation crew spending more time fixing that problem than installing the rod.

Post op is being a real fuss too, with oxygen bottle and extra drugs and infusions and a transfusion too. Oh boy!

But I'm on the mend and everything is well.

(Uh, not really *everything*, but we should be outta the hospital tomorrow. All the pain meds are working GREAT.

Just another day in MM-ville.

And so it goes and so it goes.

Comments:

> *Bruce - been thinking about you and wondering how you are... Miss your posts and hoping your recovery is still on track (the Bruce track!)*

> *Thanks for the update. So sorry you had complications. Best wishes for a continued recovery that goes smoothly!*

Femur and Fat Follow-Up

September 14, 2019

The previous "Where's Bruce" entry had our hapless MM traveler (ugh, that would be me) in hospital getting an orthopedic "nail" placed in his left femur bone to add much needed support due to damage done by a tumor. A simple, easy procedure.

Well, it seems I doesn't do nothin' easy.

(Didn't Tina Turner make that claim just before she broke into the hard rockin', sweat poppin', beat poundin' part of "Proud Mary?")

I'll veer off course just a bit and relate that during my pre-surgery "sit" with the doc I did tell her that ole Bruce... just like TT... doesn't do nothin' the easy way: SCT they told me originally "three weeks in hospital and complications were rare." "Uh, nope" says I, and I was in hospital for 53 days... permanent loss of all vision in my left eye... oops... from a "rare" form of infection.

Then there was the clinical trial earlier this year, where I was told a two day hospital stay would be required to start things off, since it was a FIH (first in human) trial, and the mice that had previously been give this new whiz-bang idea to treat MM weren't giving up much on how it might work on me.

That hospital stay stretched to seven days due to an unexpected but rare "complication."

Oh, oh… and last year there was that "move him out of ER to observe overnight" that stretched to four nights .

Are we seeing a common theme here yet?

So when the surgeon tells me they will release me "next day" I sez "Ha! No way!" punctuated with a well-placed "Bolderdash!"

We agreed to disagree.

We promptly got our first "complication" which slid our op time from Friday morning to Friday afternoon.

Do you get where this is heading?

So while in surgery here comes the "rare complication" that sent the monkey out searching for a wrench to throw.

There's even a name for the complication AND an abbreviation:

FES.

Fat Embolism Syndrome.

Here's my understanding of FES: In some surgeries like those involving big bones… like, say, a big femur on a tall male… there's a slight chance that some fat in the bone can get displaced… now this is rare, remember... some fat gets displaced into the bloodstream.

You can WIKI "fat embolism syndrome" for all the fun details, but the skinny on this fat problem... (Hee hee. Get it? 'Skinny' on this 'fat' problem!! It's a 'yuck a minute here in MM-ville tonight!)

Anyway, sans all the details... the skinny is that fat in the bloodstream of say, the lungs or the heart, or the brain, causes all sorts of alarms to go alarming and beeps and lights to be set off in the OR currently being occupied by yours truly.

And that means that the "simple nail into the femur thang" gets turned into a "Prep patient for the ICU just in case thang."

Remember, Bruce doesn't do nothin' easy.

Thanks to all the docs knowing EXACTLY how to handle the situation, ICU was not necessary.

However, you guessed it, I was not to be released "next day."

Or the next day after that, either.

Or the next day after that, either.

Tuesday rolls around, the hospital needs the bed for someone new, and I'm outta there headed for home to deal with FES residual issues and, oh yeah, that new 14" of titanium screwed into my femur bone.

The leg doesn't hurt much if I remember to dose with the Oxy. I'll soon go to just Kane - tossing Walker aside - and after that I'll break up with ol' friend Kane.

FES right now means a very, very occasional searching for the next word I want to say. Friends notice I'm doing that, and claim they will still be my friends. Hmmmm, we'll see.

There's a very, very occasional and slight shortness of breath thang going on; or that could just be my imagination, or there's some other word for it I can't remember just now. Please continue to be my friend. Okay? Please?

Psssst... psssst. But here's the really EXCITING NEWS!!!!

Whilst all these FES and nail-in-femur thangs were going on... right there going on at the SAME TIME... right there in this tired ole body o' mine, my blood count numbers are a doing the RALLY THANG!!! (It's the red hat and LOTS of prayers being said, yep yep.)

More about that once I'm better rested and back to nailing the MM instead of my femur bone.

And so it goes and so it goes.

Shots and Clots (Or Not)
October 4, 2019

Ok boys and girls, I'd like to introduce you to my new nighttime routine that's all part of keeping me safe.

This time I'm being kept safe from the dreaded "blood clots after surgery" threat.

Here's the plan... brilliant in its simplicity:

Introduce a drug (it's called Enoxaparin) into my bloodstream for the thirty days following the surgery, and Bob's your uncle (Google BYU ... it's what they say in the UK)... and BYU, no blood clots. AMAZING!

Simple.

"Uh, not so fast, Mr. Morgan... the nurse will be in to TRAIN YOU on how YOU administer this drug TO YOURSELF."

Say What???

So in trots the nurse waving this slightly smaller than expected syringe with my name on it (or at least one of the names I'll answer to)... this one sez 'Morton...' she shows me the syringe... makes it go click... pinches some of my belly fat... then stabs me... pushes rather quickly on the yellow plungy a piece...

it bottoms out and reports same with a nice authoritative click... no hurt... no blood.

They send me home with twenty-nine more doses that I administer myself right in my own pinched-by-me belly fat.

(Even Dog Ellie looks confused.)

Now my question for y'all : who among you would have difficulty doing the dirty with ol' Mr. Enoxaparin and his handy li'l administering syringe?

Doing it yourself... (Those of you who are making up sexual innuendo jokes here, SHAME ON YOU!!!)

The first five times were rough for me. I didn't do as the nurse demonstrated. It's a stab thing, and that... for me at least... was hard to accept. So I didn't stab, I sorta got to ground zero and I thought a gentle "push" was the way go.

Nope.

As in love and blood clot syringes, sometimes the stab will hurt a lot less... the stab... do it to yourself , announce your presence with authority (movie watchers alert: identify the movie.)

So... would your mind let you "self-administer" with a "stab?"

Excuse me. I'm of to Dreamland after I self-administer.

And so it goes and so it goes.

Comments:

Lol, have done it every night for the last 9 months with no end in sight!! My stomach looks like a polka dot factory!! I also started out with the slow plunge, took me a while to realize the fast jab hurts so much less!! Good luck my friend!!

Humor with all the pain and suffering = adequate survival mode! Best to you Bruce, and all us so called "warriors"! Hopefully LIVE IN TO A CURE!

I had a blood clot (DVT) in 1980 during my 3rd pregnancy, and had to give myself Heparin shots every day for nine months! It gets easier.

I couldn't do that. Had to have anyone do Neupogen 😄 😄

Good for you, Bruce Morton 👍 🎀 😎

SparkCures

Let SparkCures find a Multiple Myeloma trial for you!
SparkCures.com | 888-828-2206

Prayer!

October 7, 2019

I just came in from my front porch where my good friend Sid prayed for me. Wow! That man can pray! You know the type. Chills down my spine, complete with all my compressed vertebrae.

And Amen.

And so it goes and so it goes.

Amen…

Amen…

Amen!

Comments:

> *Prayer is SO powerful! I also have a compression fracture. Prayers to you, fellow warrior.* 🖤🖐
>
> *Amen…that is wonderful. I do believe in the power of prayer. You are so lucky and blessed to have someone praying for you like that.* 🖤🖤🖤🖤
>
> *That was the "anointing" from the Holy Spirit….good things are about to happen. Praise God!*

Trials, and So Forth

October 10, 2019

Friends came over today... Chinese carryout was carried in and it was decided not to sing, "Happy Trials to You" celebrating my signing up on the clinical trial to help bring the new MM drug Belantamab Mafodotin to market.

(Chinese food wasn't going to go down right, so I opted to just nibble and nobody noticed. Ellie dog dined richly tonight.)

This is my second Phase 1 trial and already we are veering from every plan we set up.

Trials are a work in progress, so at any time the trial sponsor (in my case drug company GlaxoSmithKline) will call and request an additional test.

That means I'll need to shimmy my pale butt to the Cancer Center to give up another vial of the red stuff.

Yesterday they drew 14 vials, and today I was told one was added; so, my first stop will be the Cancer Center for the 10 a.m. draw.

Also yesterday was an echocardiogram and my third BMB (Bone Marrow Biopsy) this year. (And I'm still a few months to go, so the sure bet is that I'll get to four yet this year.)

Trial sponsors want that baseline BMB number, so be aware that a BMB or two is just part of the trial journey. They dosed me with Demerol and it was quite an easy experience, though I would have much preferred being at home watching "The Price is Right."

"That's right nurse. Port draw."

"What's say, nurse? You like the red hat? Yeah, we are in a clinical trial and RED is the victory color. My red frame eyeglasses are on the way."

And so it goes and so it goes...

Comments:

> *Red for blood too. Thanks for keeping us updated. Prayers for a smooth process. The Price is Right isn't my style. I've been marathon watching Marvel Agents of SHIELD, on Netflix. LOL*

> *Bruce, I always said BMB's feel like you've been kicked in the a** by a mule. After 3 in one year, you, friend, are the mule! Those BMB's should be afraid. I love your tenacity and humor, always humor. I'm with you every step of the way.* ❤❤ *LOL*

BMB!

October 11, 2019

Bone marrow biopsy... the BMB.

I had my third this year just yesterday, and the episode was sort of a yawn, really. Yep. That's wha' um sayin'.

Now it didn't used to be that way with me and the fabled BMB.

I've had six BMB's while traveling the MM journey, and really only the first two hurt much at all. And that was totally my fault... I was a BMB rookie and an MM moron when it came to avoiding pain.

Those first two BMB's were given sans any anesthesia, and believe what you hear, Bunky, a BMB sans anesthesia will light you up!

So just don't do that. Have a driver to come along and get you home. And request anesthesia. They gave me IV Ativan and Demerol.

I was awake and I had a too-chatty nurse/tech that thought it was important for me to know what sensation was headed my way next throughout the entire procedure.

"Ok now you'll feel a cramping down the leg. " Whoa. And she was right! And I'll admit it was like the sweet warbling of a wren to hear: "Ok, Mr. Morgan... I'm through."

After which I'm stuck on Band-Aid Brand cuz Band-Aid stuck on me... my skinny butt plopped in the too-wide wheelchair and my caregiver and sister Karen proceeds to ram me in to the first door jamb nearby.

Next day no tender lump, not even any evidence of the procedure.

Just remember, boys and girls, to request anesthesia when you have a BMB.

I came home. Wobbled into my barely-living living room and fell fast asleep and dreamed of a new love interest...

And so it goes and so it goes...

Comments:

> *Anesthesia is the Bomb Diggity... and a MUST for BMB!!! Glad you have no nasty reminders of the procedure! Hang in there my Bud... Love & Hugs!* ☺
>
> *Don't ya wish they could put a cast on or a big sign on your shirt? A little band aid doesn't shout "Ouchiewawa!"*

I always have them put me fully asleep for mine at Moffitt. We go thru enough pain as-is.

I keep wondering if I'm getting the right procedure cuz my BMB's were so pain-free. Both done by Dr.'s at the VA (but with Dana-Farber onco fellows)... both really took a lot of time doing a lot of injections of numbing juice. Maybe that's the difference. Numbing injection, wait. More numbing, a few more minutes letting it take effect. More numbing, another few minutes. Etc. I know I have more of these in my future and hoping they go the same way.

Well Bruce I've had 15 to date, one was done using a drill, and as far as I'm concerned anesthesia works for me! 👍

Did they put a red band aid on it, to keep with your red attire?

St. Jude Children's Research Hospital

ALSAC • Danny Thomas, Founder

Finding cures. Saving children.

Drat! Scratch the Trial ☹

October 12, 2019

Well, it appears that I am no longer eligible for that quite promising clinical trial I've been telling you all about.

Lucy pulled back the football, and Charlie Brown fell on his backside.

As I was completing all the screening tests...blood draws... EKG... echocardiogram... bone marrow biopsy... my "Absolute Neutrophil" hit the skids. We don't know why, but it went from 1.7 on Tuesday to 1.1 on Wednesday to 0.5 yesterday and we had to intervene with Neupogen shots.

Neupogen shots are a no-no when trying to qualify for a clinical trial.

I'll find out on Monday what my options are. Perhaps I can wait the required two weeks and yet still get in the trial after taking the Neupogen shots. Perhaps I can return to Kyprolis/Pomalyst which was stopped a couple of weeks ago as a requirement for the trial. Perhaps we will be introduced to yet another new therapy. Perhaps...

And so it goes, and so it goes.

Keeping the Plates Spinning
October 14, 2019

Return to your childhood for just a moment. It's Sunday evening and you are, like most Americans, tuned in to the Ed Sullivan Show on TV.

The "act" to recall just now is the "plate spinner" act that was simply a guy spinning plates at the end of a long flexible rod. A series of these spinning plates all in a row... accompanied by nervous music as one plate after another juuuuust almost falls only to be rescued by the skill of the plate spinner guy.

That's my life. I'm the plate at the end of the stick that juuuust almost falls and comes crashing down.

But no. My plate spinner guy – My MM specialist – steps in to rescue me and gives that rod a gentle twist; and for a few brief moments I'm back to smooth spinning.

Ever so brief moments and my "spin" becomes all wobbly and uncomfortable to witness again.

So, just a day ago it appeared I was declared ineligible for that important clinical trial I was trying to qualify for.

My plate had taken on a death wobble.

Over the weekend however my MM specialist ordered up Neupogen shots for me. He all but assured me that a slot in the trial would be there for me on 10/28 if we can juuuuust keep my ANC number high enough to qualify so that the next day... 10/29... I can get infused with the trial drug

Folks my ANC plate is a wobblin'...

Wobblin' also is the plate that represents my platelet count. And we have a two week wait before final acceptance into the trial.

Cue the nervous music.

I've not received a treatment for my MM now for three weeks, so as would be expected Mr. Myeloma is kicking the heck out of my hemo count. I'm at just 8.4. I'm one tired, tired fellow MM traveler, but I'm encouraged that on the 28th I'll deliver up sufficient counts to make the cut for the trial.

I'm discovering that this clinical trial game is a numbers game and a plate spinning act.

And so it goes and so it goes

Comments:

Prayers for the number!

This is going to happen!! It has to... ♥

Cherie

October 26, 2019

I'm sad. Very sad at the passing of our friend Cherie Rineker.

Just days before she left for Colorado, she offered sage advice to me about my MM journey. I'd just been denied the opportunity to get in to a promising clinical trial.

What was next coming up behind that?

Cherie's journey and my MM journey shared some similarities. We both got our SCT in August of 2013. We both wore out therapies rapidly. My "next" therapy this year will be my fourth "line" since March.

Only one of those therapy lines "worked," and I chose to cut that one short and take a shot at a clinical trial that might have worked on me. And... and this is what captured my interest... my participation in the trial would move the drug along in the FDA approval process.

On the eve of entry into the trial... inexplicably... my ANC went from 1.7 to 0.5. That meant I had to be given Neupogen shots. That meant the trial sponsors were now saying "No" to me.

Cherie knew what it was like to hear that "no" and her words were a comfort to me: "In this MM game when you get bucked off the pony, you stand... brush yourself off... and put your hope in a 'next' therapy."

With Cherie's passing all of us are sad... we got bucked off the pony and hit the ground hard.

What now?

We stand... brush ourselves off... and get right back into it.

Those who can, should consider searching out a clinical trial to be their "next" therapy so those coming up behind them afflicted with MM will have more choices along their MM journey.

What then for me?

Well my doc immediately brushed me off... three shots of Neupogen... two transfusions... perhaps more on Monday. Retesting.

It ain't over 'til it's over! We are gonna turn a "no" into a "yes".

I find out on Tuesday if our second go at the clinical trial for new GSK drug Belantamab Mafodotin is successful.

Folks, this is OUR trial. We work as a team to work as one force against MM.

Sad though I am, it's time to get back on that pony, eh?

And so it goes, and so it goes.

Comments:

> Get on and Ride the hell out of it!! I hope and pray that this works out for you!

> Yes, dismayed by Cherie's final "treatment", when she traveled such an incredible MM journey, achieving so much advocacy. I wish and hope a foundation is created to continue her advocacy and mentoring! I also send much positivity for this clinical trial for you; that you are finally accepted and it works well! For you and all of us! I'm a nine year survivor, so far. Keep the journey going. LIVE IN TO A CURE.

> Don't lose hope Bruce. Cherie Rineker is up there in heaven egging you on. You're a warrior and a toughie, keep up the hard work for yourself and everyone else. You're carrying on Cherie's legacy
> Great post! Thank you, friend ♥

> Beautifully said. Thank you, Bruce.

It Is Well!

October 26, 2019

Did you know!? The song, "It Is Well With My Soul" was written by a successful Christian lawyer Horatio Spafford. His only son died at age 4 in 1871. In 1872, the great Chicago fire wiped out his vast estate, made from a successful legal career. In 1873 he sent his wife and 4 daughters over to Europe on a summer trip on the ill-fated SS Ville du Havre. Since he had a lot of work to do, he planned to follow them later. The ship sank and he lost his 4 daughters with the wife being the only survivor. She sent him a famous telegram which simply read, "SAVED ALONE..." On his return home, his law firm was burned down and the insurance company refused to pay him. They said "It's an Act of God." He had no money to pay for his house, no work, and he also lost his house. Then while sitting and thinking about what was happening to him, being a spiritual person, he wrote a song: "Whatever, my Lord, You have taught me to say, It is well, it is well with my soul." My dear friend, a good attitude will determine your altitude. When you look at your life, career, job or family life, what do you say? Do you praise God? Do you blame the devil? A good attitude towards God makes Him move on your behalf. Just sit down and say, "Today, God, it is well with my soul, I am thankful I had a peaceful sleep, I am thankful I am alive with possibilities, I am thankful I have a roof over me, I am thankful I have a job, I am thankful that I have Family and Friends. Above all, I am thankful that I have the Lord Jesus Christ on my side." Be blessed and don't be envious or shocked when others are prospering because you don't know what they have been through to get there (test, trials and tribulation) so thank God for what you have. "Little is much when God is in it. It Is Well With My Soul!" Touch someone's life with this message. If God is for us, who can be against us? A blessing is coming your way, my friend!! ❤

My fav hymn, and I drive a Kia Soul with an "It Is Well With My Soul" decal on the back window.

I'm IN!

October 29, 2019

YES! Bruce has been accepted into the GSK2857916 DREAMM6 clinical trial.

Those of you who follow my posts here will recall that a little over two weeks ago I was not eligible for this trial because my ANC suddenly dropped, and when we swooped in with Neupogen shots we were required to wait two weeks sans any additional Neupogen.

Today's test revealed that my ANC held up to the testing by a good margin.

But just to keep things interesting my platelets gave us bit of a "close call" testing at just 76 – just one above the required 75! Whew!

So I was "in," and I can begin the challenge of staying "in." And dodging a pesky side effect: blurry vision.

In previous Phase 1 trials on GSK2857916 there was a 70% incidence of the layers of the cornea developing air pockets causing blurry vision.

This side effect is particularly troubling to me because I only have vision in my right eye.

Yep. I lost all vision... permanently... in my left eye due to an infection during my SCT in 2013.

Yikes, Bruce, you only have one working eyeball, and yet you enter a trial that we pretty much know will blur your vision? What are you, nuts?!

Perhaps I've positioned myself a bit "futher" (that's Cape Girardeau speak... it means "further." Drop the "r," big city boy.) futher out on the limb.

However, I've already had my first appointment with the eye doctor, and they are monitoring my one remaining eye very close. I'll be fine.

Today's first infusion was not without incident, though. About half way through the thirty-minute infusion, I began itching and my face got red and blotchy. And a sort of fever blister erupted on my lip. However, 50mg of Benadryl solved that lickety-split.

So hooray, I'll be helping bring this drug to market and I'm hearing they might be able to come with this brand new drug in a brand new class of MM therapies perhaps in 2019. That's right around the corner folks. Exciting, eh?

We'll tame the blurry vision side effect.

And, I'm in an arm of the study that teams the GSK drug with Dex and Velcade. So we may be stirring up a brand new therapy that is well tolerated and sends bad guy MM cell a-packin'.

As they tell me more about GSK2857916 I'll share that with you, and I'll reveal my campaign to secure naming rights to yours truly: The new drug, once out of trial, will be called "Bruce Juice."

And so it goes. And so it goes.

Comments:

FANTASTIC! So happy, glad, excited, relieved, forward-looking to the availability of another treatment. Hope it works for you. Hope it goes well. Hope it comes to FDA market. Thank you for doing a clinical trial. Thank you for your humor. Thank you for posting your continuing experiences. Thank you for staying alive! Thank you for sharing. Sorry about your eye and eyes. Smile. Laugh. Cry. Breathe. Remember to LIVE IN TO A CURE!

So pleased for you Bruce!! X

That's a great bit of news right there Bruce!!! 🖐 Glad they have you In There and pray that it works for you with little side effects. 🙏 I love the name "Bruce Juice" 😊 let's see if they incorporate your name in the drug. 😆😆😆😆. Keep up the good fight!! We got this!!!! 💪

Oh my goodness, Congratulations Bruce!! So very happy to read this news!! Sending out a boatload of positive thoughts and well wishes for you!!

I'm very happy for you Bruce!!! I wish you well in this clinical trial and hope "Bruce Juice" will be in the MM arsenal soon. And, hope the side effects are minimal, for God is good all the time.

So happy for you Bruce.

St. Jude Children's Research Hospital

ALSAC • Danny Thomas, Founder

Finding cures. Saving children.

Therapy the Sixth
October 30, 2019

Ugh. Part of my new therapy includes Dex, so I'll not get much sleep tonight.

Here it is then...

Think back to Herman's Hermits, and this is their tribute song to MM. Or, maybe not...

Remember the *Henry the 8th* tune?

Google it:

> I'm therapy the sixth, I am
>
> Therapy the sixth, I am, I am.
>
> I got into a clinical trial
>
> Just to try to make this sick man smile.
>
> And every line was so promising,
>
> We scared that Myeloma every time!
>
> I'm this boy's sixth line of therapy.
>
> Therapy the sixth, I am, I am,
>
> Therapy the sixth I am.
>
> Second verse, same as the first!

Now you KNOW you will be singing your best Hermits songs all day today. Smile now, eh.

Right now the line of therapy you are in is the PERFECT line to go at your personal MM challenge. Today your line of therapy (or maybe you are off therapy for now) your line is perfect and chosen to work for you. Be encouraged, yeah!

And so it goes. And so it goes.

Comments:

I took my DEX last night (I usually take it early in the morning) but I forgot yesterday was Tuesday ☺

Dex never kept me from sleeping. Guess I'm just weird lol...

Love the new tune. Let's pray 6 is your lucky number.

I went to bed with this song in my head.

Yes, I do remember the song. A friend of mine and I sang it all the time. Now your version is more entertaining and does hit home. I somehow think your sleepless night won't be a lost cause.

Lol I sang it Good Luck and God Bless.

Thankfulness

November 9, 2019

Thankful I am, boy howdy...

I'm not into Thanksgiving Day yet, and I'll not have much to do with Black Friday, methinks.

This is just me steeped in gratitude for the many blessings I'm enjoying. Yeah, steeped in gratitude.

With the help of so many others I navigated through a host of assaults from my MM this year. My MM is advancing at every opportunity, and we've had to adjust to this.

We've used up the "off the shelf" FDA approved lines of treatment. It's a different journey now. If this were tennis, I'd remark that MM now has the "advantage".

Tipping Point. Bent towards MM and away from me.

What to do then? If this is a game, the rules have changed.

I hate change. Always have.

And what's going on now are truly LIFE changing and LIFE threatening.

All too well all of us know our common fate once our MM specialist has to reach deeper into his bag of tricks.

The loss of Cherie Rineker and others to MM in recent weeks shook me. It brought the reality of the dark side of this affliction heavy onto me. Heavy stuff, eh.

I personally try to move opposite to the dark places.

I can and I will dwell in my "happy go lucky" persona. That dark stuff just gets stuffed away, I say.

Which brings me to an update on this clinical trial I'm in. Yippee!! So far, so good. On Tuesday they will drain some of my red stuff and measure my Lambda Light Chain count and I'm bettin' this new trial drug is giving ol' MM bit of a surprise.

Ha! Red rally cap is on. Red shoes say, "I'm in this journey... ALL IN... new rules and all." We offer our self to the unknowns in each new trial drug.

Be watching for my updates on this one that's coursing through me now... it's a good one... GSK2857916!

And so it goes, and so it goes.

Comments:

Bruce my friend!! Glad you're doing good and back to writing. I know this GSK#### will do wonders for you. 😁 We are all struggling with this dag nabbit MM and we feel ya, it can take a toll. Know we are here for a boost in the ole morale department. 💪 Tell Ellie to play tug-o-war with you. Oh wait, frisbee instead.

Look forward to each of your updates, Bruce Morton! Red rally cap On!

Yep, 💪💪💪 makes all the difference.

Hang in there, Bruce. You have a lot of us rallying for you and wishing you all the best in this trial. Keep us posted.

And so it goes. And so it goes.

Let SparkCures find a Multiple Myeloma trial for you!
SparkCures.com | 888-828-2206

Garage Therapy
November 22, 2019

I just spent $400 to pay a mechanic to fix my vintage 1971 British sports car, and I'm not making this up... I'm considering that spend as a health care "cost."

Huh? What?

I've owned that car for a lot of years, and *always* did *all* the work myself...

Then I began my journey with MM. I lost my ability to crawl into that low-slung sled. I lost my strength to the MM... no more air-ratcheting off the lug nuts, because I couldn't bend low where lug nuts live, and if I was foolish enough to try I certainly could not get myself standing again so I could trudge back to my recliner in my barely-living living room. So I rested and recovered on the garage floor and had to "put up" the LBC... Little British Car.

That was 7 years ago. Once... just once, about three years ago, I tried... and failed miserably to start the car.

I'd owned and restored many LBC's, but chemo brain has taken up residence in my cranium such that all my knowledge of how to fix stuff – especially a 50 year old car – is just ga-ga-gone. After several failed goes at stomping at the MM and getting SPANKED and HARD by my travel partner on this journey, the MM, I didn't try again.

But just recently however... since mid-September... I got patched up just enough that I decided to take another run at going zoom-zoom in my LBC.

Thanks to chemo brain I'm no longer toting any smarts as to how put a fix on the car so I happily paid a mechanic that $400.

And now I can sit in the LBC, AND wrestle my way up and out of it. That was a real chore, so today my brother Mike and I rigged up a rope to the garage ceiling... It's a struggle, but I can now pull up and kick my way out. Egress.

Ha! MM... in your face... the tumors this summer got radiation treatment.

Ha! Surgical placement of a support rod in my femur. I can kick and stand up now.

Ha! Just when we were 'bout out of lines of treatment against the MM, I get in a clinical trial that's punching back at it. And THAT means HOPE has joined in the party.

Hope.

Yeah we MUST KEEP our hope alive.

Perhaps revisiting something enjoyable that we had to temporarily "put up." Hope allows us to step back to some of our enjoyments before all this new normal happened upon us.

I'm still sick a lot. Fatigue set me to the horizontal position all day on Monday.

But on Tuesday I played zoom in my LBC. Crawled out. Barely. Then three doses of steroid eye drops that are part of the trial.

Tomorrow is all day at the Cancer Center trying to jump-start production of my platelets. Transfusion? Yeah, probably.

And so it goes . And so it goes.

Comments:

Absolutely! You must have those victorious moments!!

Three cheers for HOPE! Bet you look snappy in that car. ☺

Bruce Morton I love your attitude!! Love that you are enjoying your LBC again! And the best part is HOPE!!! Thanks for the chuckles and joy your words brought to me today ♥ *Keep on keeping on!*

For some of us a trial can be a right good thing . Ask your MM specialist, or go to Sparkcures to search out a trial.

Adventures With Gravity

November 9, 2019

"Are you going to post on Facebook about your shopping trip to Harbor Freight?" ... that said by sister and primary caregiver, my sister Karen.

"Sure. Why not? Makes for a good yarn and it's this pesky MM that caused the whole incident right there in public view."

"Go for it" she coaxed, as she enjoys it when I never seem to skip a day without some sort of calamity. Oh well...

Okay, okay... here goes. This clinical trial I'm in requires me to combo the new and promising drug with my old friend, daddy Dexamethasone. Ugh.

I'd been off that steroid for quite a long time... at least a year.

But now I dose on Tuesday, Wednesday, Friday, and Saturday. So I don't sleep. But also IMMEDIATELY I gain weight. I pork up around my middle but not around my waist. 34 waist stays the same but I get a Buddha belly that my pants can't climb up over... 42... then 44... whoops, 46 and beyond. I'll eventually keep the pants hoisted up to the newly formed belly with suspenders. (And I yell this mean yell: "Hey you kids GET OFF MY LAWN!!") You get the picture.

So I get frisky and go to the Harbor Freight store and EVERYTHING in that store to buy is WAY HEAVIER than I can lift.

(Spoiler alert... I'm not wearing my suspenders.)

I'm after a folding work benchy thingy that is inconveniently located about face high on a shelf for strong and healthy shoppers, and I am no longer of that group. Alas.

Undeterred I reach up and give the thing a yank, and I'm surprised by how suddenly the box of bench lands fully into my control. Sadly, "control" of heavy stuff ain't what I do... I fumble and try not to get hurt mostly with anything remotely heavy.

So I'm putting on the WWF wrestle to Heavy Benchy Thingy and my non-suspendered pants immediately drop to my ankles.

Phoom!

But Heavy doesn't want to be returned to his shelf spot. More wrestling, only this time I'm even less suited to do the dance because my pants are hindering free movement down by my feets.

Yes. There were other shoppers in the store

No. They offered no assistance .

Eventually I get Heavy home. I check out using the 20% Off coupon and head for home to locate my suspenders.

And so it goes... and so it goes.

Comments:

> *That sure made me chuckle. (But I was laughing with you, not at you). Thanks for the day brightener, Bruce.* 💜
>
> *Does everyone get weight gain with steroids?*
>
> *I'm right there with ya. Once while on some med that caused my weight to fluctuate, my skirt feel to my feet. Of course I had to be in the parking lot of an art museum in the hoity-toity part of Tulsa. Mighty glad I'm not a regular at that museum.*
>
> *Ohhhh Lordy!! Get those suspenders quick!!! And I'm glad you were not hurt!*
>
> *Oh wow!! That's a picture! I was on a plane ✈ once where a guy was wrestling his suitcase into an overhead bin and yep... his has pants fell to his ankles! He was able to throw the suitcase in quick and then pick up his pants 👖 that had settled around his ankles! 😁 Everyone was clapping!!*

Lowering the Lambda
November 19, 2019

Bruce: "Alexa, temperature!"

Alexa: "Right now In Creve Coeur, Missouri, it's 35 degrees Fahrenheit."

Bruce: "Alexa, what is my Lambda Light Chain marker number?"

Alexa: "How should I know? You never share your numbers with me."

Bruce: "Okay, okay. I'll tell you this time. There's a bit of backstory, A-girl... see, I'm in a clinical trial to help develop a new MM drug. The drug is given in combo with Velcade and Dex. I took the first dose of this combo on October 28, and a second dose on November 4. All year my Lambda Light Chain marker had been rising: early October 55, mid October 83, early November, (gulp) 128. Ok Alexa, take a guess what the LLC marker is right now... after two doses of the trial combo, what's my number?"

Alexa: "You sound perky... I'll guess it dropped to... to uh... to 100."

Bruce: "Nope. Right now I'm way below that... to a number that's almost too low to believe. Yep, two doses of the drug, and I'm back to a very encouraging LLC number.

Wow and wow!

There's a problem, however.

My platelets are going down, down, down, so I'm getting transfusions for that. If the platelets don't settle, I'll be looked at as a not-so-ideal participant in the trial, and might have trouble remaining.

So for now we celebrate the low marker number... lowest it's been this entire year.

And I'm going to learn more about this GSK2857916 trial drug, and I'll share all that I learn with our FB groups.

And so it goes and so it goes.

Comments:

Great news about those light chains!!! Platelets need to get with the program... sending hugs.

I'm doing a trial drug at Dana Farber for going on four years now; ACE111 I believe it's called; to bring my platelets up from the Revlimid making them drop so low. I too have Lambda Light Chain.

Thanksgiving

November 28, 2019

There shall be no negative thoughts this day.

Our default setting is to be positive today and beyond.

"What's Bruce so happy about? I thought he had cancer?" They will think that about me, and that's what I want this day.

I want to ease THEIR concerns about me and my MM journey.

Pain?

What pain?

Pass the gravy, please.

Why not this day give 'em what they want?

What those around the table want, besides 'Where's moms Jell-o salad?'... what they want for us is some relief.

So I'll show it this way today.

"I'm fine Mom. Pass the gravy, please."

And so it goes and so it goes.

Comments:

That is the sweetest thing I ever read, and a wonderful gift to give your family!

Have a blessed day, Bruce. We always have things for which to be thankful.

Happy Thanksgiving to all from Australia.

A blessed Thanksgiving to you. I haven't told my family yet. I'm not 100% yet. Waiting on blood work. I smiled, I laughed, and I passed the gravy.

What a good son. I feel the same way. I want to remember that part of giving thanks is to help others give thanks.

Let SparkCures find a Multiple Myeloma trial for you!
SparkCures.com | 888-828-2206

Wonderfulness

November 30, 2019

Whoa diggy! Now THAT was a wonderful Thanksgiving!

It was such a blessing to be with my ace caregiver... my sister Karen... and we agreed beforehand to focus on all we had to be thankful for.

My 94-year-old mother gave me such a sweet kiss on the cheek...

The days of the womenfolk toiling all day on the big family meal while the menfolk watch football are behind us.

The extended family is scattered about now... there was just five us.

So the $9.99-per-person carry-out turkey dinner from the local grocery was nuked... beep beep beep... done!

Pssst pssst. Little secret... the turkey was fabulous. I'm pretty sure they brined the bird... juicy... tender...

And each person got a reasonably sized serving... no after meal "I ate too much" groans.

We all agreed to carry the "Thankful" theme on throughout this "Holiday" season. No hustle bustle.

Yeah. Thankful.

My Black Friday evening was spent at the Cancer Center because of my platelet count that seemed stuck in the teens. Would I need another bag of platelets, or two?

Nope.

28 is a low count but there was no need to infuse me, so at 9 p.m. they sent me home.

The other counts are ok. We will get another dose of the clinical trial drug on Tuesday. Dex and Velcade for dessert.

And so it goes and so it goes.

Comments:

Happy Thanksgiving! We did the same, ordered from Cracker Barrel. Our usual 50 peeps was only 30, so... but the relief of stress and hours on the feet was wonderful! My dad was so happy his kiddos had a stress-free day. #grateful.

It's so good to be thankful! I am thankful for getting to know you Bruce, even if it took Myeloma to bring us together 👍 ❤️ 🤗

Nicely worded. I love your thoughts about your "new" Thanksgiving. Flexibility is key. And, I appreciate your tip about your Turkey dinner. Keep up the good fight.

"And so it goes, and so it goes"... love it!

I'm guessing your line was a lot shorter than other lines on Black Friday, and no fights broke out over the last bag of platelets.

Thankful! ♪♪♪♪

Yes, am also focusing on being thankful. Just had my son & granddaughter here early on Thursday. Got lots of love, did not eat too much & took a two hour nap later in afternoon. It was perfect, I am blessed 💙

St. Jude Children's Research Hospital

ALSAC • Danny Thomas, Founder

Finding cures. Saving children.

Mole-Whacking, and So Forth
November 30, 2019

Ha!

Now I'll admit I'm more of a "dog person" than "cat person," but I did get a chuckle from the newest infomercial making the rounds on late night TV (uh... oops... it wharn't late night, it were early early morning and I was juiced on Dex...)

The back story is that I've been known to compare MM to a "Whack-a-Mole" game... like at a carnival.

You get me; as soon as we go a'figurin' we know what's a-coming next with our MM, up pops some ailment we never considered.

Whaaaaa. Me?

I'll say the 14" titanium bar put in my left femur wasn't originally part of my September plan for 2019.

Whack a Mole. Hee hee.

For cats this holiday season, they are pitching the "Pop And Play" toy as a rollicking good time for kitty... fun fun... and I'm not making this up... *it's just like the Whack-a-Mole game!*

Really? Listen up tabby cat, Whack-a-Mole is an exercise in frustration.

At least the way I play it...

Hereeeeeere, kitty kitty.

Google *Pop and Play* for Cats... there's still time to get delivery before Christmas I'll bet!

And so it goes and so it goes

Comments:

My cat loves his "Whack-a-Mole!"

You're right about MM being like that. I decided from day 1 that I needed to approach this with a sense of humor. It's the only way to survive the BS it deals us. I can't win the bloody Lotto, but I ended up with both MM and MDS... ☺ Oh well, that's life! I learned long ago from being married to a farmer that you have to approach things you can't control with a sense of humor. If you don't, you'll die from the stress it creates. 2019 handed us the wettest spring on record, which delayed or prevented our crops from being planted, and then we had a drought over the summer. Now all it does is rain or snow, so what crops we did get planted we're unable to harvest because it's too wet.

My daughter just got the Pop and Play *for her kitty, and she loves it. But, I am and always will be a dog person. Both my daughters have recently gotten cats for their families and try to convince me to get one. No thanks.* ☺

Clots? Lots? We're Hoping Not

December 6, 2019

Platelets circling the drain at just 28. All my other counts are encouraging; it's da platelets.

> I'm part of the no clot lot.
> It's not easy to spot just a dot dat don't,
> Don't clot
> No got clot at that spot
> Well, it is red...
> But that being said...
> See
> The thing is,
> It don't clot
> When it should,
> Should clot
> A should-clot becomes a not-clot-spot.
> They hangs a bag to get the count up.
> But once a true "clot-not" shows up for a draw down drama dips then drags.
> See, I'm part of the no clot lot.

And so it goes and so it goes.

Dr. Bruce Seuss ☺☺

Comments:

> Me too. Have you been checked for Von Wildebrand's disease? Found out that was my problem (still is).
>
> Stay sitting or lying down so you don't fall!
>
> Right. Fall and crack that noggin. You can have a brain bleed easily that can be fatal.
>
> How much blood would a "clot-not" clot if a "clot-not" could clot blood? 😜
>
> Say that real fast without looking three times! This made me smile.
>
> After my SCT in 05 my platelets never got above 10,000, so it was decided to do a spleen... and 14 yrs later my platelets have dropped below 450,000.
>
> Ha ha no clot lot don't clot, say 3 times fast. Hopefully you will join the clot alot very soon.
>
> Have they checked you for a virus? Are you on antibiotics?
>
> Have they tried a platelet elevating drug?

The New Stopping Place

December 11, 2019

I'll stop when I come to "a good stopping place…" that's how I always did things… before my journey with MM.

But now there's a "new normal" that puts a throttle on how much I can do. The old "good stopping place" is quite… maybe probably… unreachable now.

So be it.

We "reset" that good stopping place.

The body says "stop now…" or "you shoulda stopped 20 minutes ago."

Reset that "good stopping place…" that old good stopping place ain't no use to me no more.

Reset it to "now Bruce."

Get back to the recliner and rehydrate. Nap. Just catch up on emails NOW.

Lay down the spoon and the spatula NOW.

Get up off the floor with the darling (bless their hearts) grandkids NOW.

I'm not as good stopping as I will be once I learn to stop to the new good stopping place. The body will tell me.

And so it goes and so it goes.

Comments:

> Ah yes, the new stopping point! Know it all too well. I just bought a bike trainer for indoors for days when I can't ride outside. Haven't tried it yet but this week it will be put to use. I pray I don't go past my stopping point.
>
> Ohhhh... the New Stopping point! Listen to your body... they can be quiet bossy!! Love & hugs my friend.
>
> There's an analogy about spoons in your drawer. Every day you have so many clean spoons. As you start your day, think about your spoons and with every activity you do recognize how many clean spoons you have to give up to finish that activity. Recognize that you have to get to the end of the day with at least one spoon. This helps you decide whether or not you were able to do certain activities or even small activities because you simply will not have enough spoons to finish the day. This helps my friend who has lupus and it helped me say no to things I normally would sing sure I could do. Spoons in the drawer, how many do you have left?

Dex Crash!

December 16, 2019

Hee hee.

After a short break from my occasional calamities linked to my MM journey I'm, "at it" once more.

The back story is that the clinical trial I'm in includes Dex dosing on four days each week, and no "rest" week.

Yikes and boy howdy, I'm quite a Dex mess most of the time.

I did not sleep a wink for forty-eight hours, so once I did crash the body needed LOTS...

So now as I piece it together, I went to the recliner... ate a snack of hot chicken wings around 10:00 last night... Yum... washed down with a too-small 7oz Bud Light...

Then the body said with a huge sigh, "OFF." And I was OUT! Chicken bones and too-small beer bottle on my lap.

Next I wake up and it's 5:50, but I had no recollection of when the body said "OFF!" Is it 5:50 a.m. or 5:50 p.m.?

It's very dark outside.

Where'd all these chicken bones come from??

I needed to pee, but that told me little about what part of the day I was dealing with.

Moved to the bedroom and at 9:00 now it was light out so that mystery was solved.

But dog Ellie was chasing thru the house which is unlike her. Turns out a bird had gotten into the house thru the doggie door I put in so Ellie could let herself in/out on Dex days when I sleep for 11 hours and wake up in a mound of chicken bones and short "long necks."

Chased the bird out. Took my morning meds.

"Alexa! Play Christmas songs by Perry Como."

And so it goes and so it goes.

Comments:

> *Oh Bruce! You amaze me. Glad you're doing good and hope those Dex days don't make you leave the door open for more than birds to come in. 😂😂😂😂 Glad Ellie got some much needed exercise though!* 😊
>
> *Bruce Morton… So always need to hear what you share. Things have been particularly difficult of late, month or so. You always put such a wonderful light on the difficult, a chuckle when it*

can be so tough. Thank you for the holiday gift I so much needed! May you too, receive something from your sharing. It is most wonderful, most wonderful!

Hate Dex!!! I have to consciously think about being nice when I want to be ugly! It's hard! Jekyll and Hyde!! Mostly Hyde...

I had a crush on Perry Como ♥

Perry has been playing here as well. Glad you were blessed with much needed ZZZZZZZZssss.

I love Mojitos with my homemade hot wings... just the right amount of mint n lime to cool the belly.

Let SparkCures find a Multiple Myeloma trial for you!
SparkCures.com | 888-828-2206

A Thought for Mike

December 22, 2019

"Hey group," as we say in my home town of Jackson MO, outside of Cape Girardeau, "We're in a pickle."

Not me this time though...

My older brother, Mike, went in last Monday for a surprise, but rather routine nowadays, quad bypass surgery.

Since then, all things that could go wonky went wonky. Second surgery to fix a tear in his aorta... The incision in his chest wasn't closed until Thursday, in case they had to get in quickly for additional repairs. Feeding tube still in, and he is mostly still sedated.

I've floated a plan with Karen, my caregiver, that despite my health issues that kobble me... that she and I squeeze in a trip to Colorado Springs from our home here in St. Louis, a 12-hour ride per Google Maps.

Mike remains in the ICU, so the trip may be ill timed... Christmas Day at the hospital... been there, done that.

And so it goes... and so it goes.

The Best-Laid Plans...

December 26, 2019

Road trip?

Not so fast, buster!

Yeah, I was a-fixin' (that's Cape Girardeau speak... it means "puttin' on the get-ready" for a hurried trip to Colorado to see my brother... he's been in ICU for nine days now. But I can't go just yet.

The back story is that brother Mike went for what is nowadays a somewhat routine quad bypass surgery. That six-hour surgery uncovered a tear in his aorta... more hours of surgery... bleeding leak that would not reveal its location... more surgeries... kidney involvement...

I want to be there but I'm not free to travel.

Fooey.

My platelet count has dropped to just 16, and I'm being infused every couple of days.

And, fooey on top of fooey and "F Bomb" alert:

Fiddlesticks! Yeah, Fiddlesticks.

We found out on Tuesday that my 94-year-old mother has to have an operation on a toe, and that means my sister Karen has to stay and tend to that situation.

So I wait until Monday to find out what we will do about my platelet shortfall.

And I ask for your prayers for brother Mike. It's been a very dangerous situation... tenth day starts tomorrow.

I want to be there. Something will work out that I can...

And so it goes and so it goes

Comments:

> *Yes Bruce, I will gladly send you and your brother any extra, plus more, healing and helping energy I have! You were so lovingly putting it out there for your brother. I will give numerous meditating moments each day to him, and you, as one strong energy. Two are stronger than one! Three, even stronger! And may calm and peaceful days come upon both of you. Just breathe, repeat.*
>
> *Prayers for all of you.*

The Plot Thickens

January 5, 2020

Whew! The grade of my MM journey has been a bit steeper of late.

A bit.

So I lurked here, rather than post.

To recap, my brother Mike found out he required quad heart bypass surgery way back on December 23. There the surgeons found a major tear to his aorta. Repair of that did not go well. Massive loss of blood. Stroke. He is still in ICU.

Prayers for him, please. He is by no means "out of the woods" yet. Each day we get news of a new and serious complication.

I was packed to make the trip out to Colorado just to be with my brother, but that so far has not been possible.

First, my 94-year-old mom requires toe amputation, so caregiver and sister Karen's attention has been diverted away from me.

Me? Well, the clinical drug I'm on is working GREAT to push down on my MM. Yippee!

The side effects though mean it's not wise for me to head west to see Mike just yet.

My platelet count is low low.

Then it went down even lower. Got down to 10. Infusions didn't have much effect.

Then there is the quite troubling blurring of my vision. As predicted, the trial drug can and regularly does cause that at cycle 3. That's exactly when this pesky side effect came to visit me.

It's not a good idea for me to drive... certainly not at night.

So I stay homebound, and dose on leftover Christmas cookies and chocolate pie. Mmmmmm.

And miss my brother.

I see the doc on Tuesday, and I'll politic to remain in the trial, hoping that a dose reduction in the stuff returns vision to my one remaining eye. (I lost all vision in my left eye 7 years ago while in for SCT. Whoops!) So, playing "chicken" with my only remaining source of vision is a bit dicey.

But folks, I'm encouraged that this drug WORKS! My Lambda Light Chain before trial was 128. Now? Just 10! Wow and Wow!

Pray for my brother Mike's recovery.

Pray that the doc and the trial sponsors let us... yes, all of us are "in" this trial together... let us stay in the trial at a safer reduced dose.

Trials are the important business of our MM journey. Work with your doc and MM team to find a right trial for you.

And so it goes and so it goes.

Comments:

> *You and your family are surely in need of prayers. You have mine! I hope things will begin to improve for all of you!*
>
> *Continued prayers and well wishes for your brother Mike, your mom, and you ❣ Thank you for your participation in the Trial, because yes, it helps the MM Community as a whole!*
>
> *You are an amazing strong warrior! 💪❤*
>
> *So much going on for you and your family right now. It amazes me sometimes how much we deal with at once.*
>
> *I'm sending healing love to your brother and your mother. I'm also sending patience to you. 💗*
>
> *God be with you all.*

Go West!

January 7, 2020

Heading west to see my brother on Saturday! Yah!

He's in a hospital in Colorado Springs on a SLOW and arduous recovery from a quad bypass surgery on December 23.

Yeah. He's been in ICU since then!

I've been working to clear a path for me to be there, and today we made huge progress

First, at the Cancer Center today, with the aid of an infusion, we got my platelet count from 19 to a just barely enough 27.

So I was able to get a dose of the trial drug, and that means starting on Saturday I'm on a "rest" week and I can travel.

Secondly there's nothing much that can be done about my blurry vision, so all I needed to do is find someone willing to drive me to CO, and by golly my friend and #1 prayer warrior on my A TEAM Brett has agreed to do the driving. (Blurry vision... a side effect of the trial drug... makes it unwise for me to drive for now)

One more hurdle cleared today; Finances. Gasoline, meals and hotel rooms aren't free. But in TODAY's MAIL came the BIG SURPRISE.

A check big enough to pay for everything!

And you'll never guess who the check came from. My health insurance company!

Whaaaaaaat? Nobody gets a check FROM the insurance company. (We figure the check is to square up all that went on with me in 2019. I was in two trials... there were three hospital stays... surgery... several high-cost drug lines.

I'd made a plea to this group and a couple other FB Private Groups just a few days ago.

The lesson???

Surround yourself with good, caring people.

Even if just a "cyber surround," it can work to make things happen.

Thanks to everyone for remembering brother Mike and me in your daily thoughts and prayers.

And so it goes, and so it goes.

The Plot Thickens... Again

January 12, 2020

"And so it goes and so it goes."

That's a chant I often choose to close a post, but at this early hour of the morning I'm awash, needing that as a remembrance this day.

I'd planned to be driven 800 miles west to see my brother Mike, who has been in ICU there since December 23. (Heart bypass complications.)

Lots and lots of prayers said, and lots and lots of prayers answered in the affirmative.

But, uh, it was not to be... travel, that is...

A snow line inched across western Missouri

Inched.

So we put off travel to Colorado Springs

And so it goes...

However!!! Shout with Praise!! All was not lost.

Around 7:00 p.m. my smart phone lit up with my brother's ring tone!!! Wow and wow!

They have moved him out of ICU, and we had the most glorious 30 second conversation two brothers could ever have... I cried then as I am right now. And so it goes.

Meanwhile, Back at the Trial

January 12, 2020

Yep yep, I'm UP all night on a mega-dose of Dex.

So how's about a clinical trial update to go with my poached eggs and cheese grits? (Here in Missouri we are juuuuust on the edge of true grits country. Ya gotta get one state futher south for the honest fixuns.)

This trial is Phase 1/2 and I'm just starting my fourth cycle.

Methinks I'll make it to the fifth cycle... then whoops, the side effects I'm experiencing might call for a break in the action.

The most troubling side effect is blurred vision in my one remaining good eye. (Yeah yeah, back in August 2013 during SCT I lost all vision in my left eye... fungal infection. Yuck!)

No big deal, really. I've driven over 100,000 miles on our nation's highways since then, and no tickets or accidents. (I'll admit, I've crashed my grocery shopping cart a few times when some shopper cuts me off as I'm reachin' for the grits.)

So for now I don't drive... day or night.

"Look Ellie, here comes the Amazon truck with your dog food."

Blurry vision makes it very hard to tap at the smart phone... watching TV is useless, and I can barely read the print on the Pillsbury brownie box with my Sherlock Holmes magnifying glass. Once we lay off this trial drug for a bit they tell me I'll be fine.

Oh, and my platelet count dipped out of range... then dipped some more just to get everyone's attention... then dipped some more, such that I get an infusion that looks like chicken soup at least once a week.

"You will be fine Mr. Morgan we never make any mistakes 😀"

Fatigue on Dex crash days... up all night at least four times a week...

Neuropathy in the feets is calling for more Gabapentin... no nausea or diarrhea.

Now at the start of cycle one, my Lambda Light Chain marker was perched at 128. Whoa! Nellie!

Some perspective: last summer when my LLC shot past 100, Mr. Plasmacytoma paid a visit to my left femur, and that required surgery.

Again I hear :"You'll be fine." (And they were right, hee hee.)

Well, fellow MM travelers, on Tuesday my LLC had dropped down to just 10! Yep just one zero behind that one... down to just 10.

So, for now I put up with the blurry vision and low platelets.

"I'll be fine, says I."

And so it goes and so it goes.

(The clinical trial I'm on is GSK2857916. You can Google it; also known as Belantamab Mafodotin.)

Comments:

Had to get platelets myself this past week. I thought of orange juice, not chicken soup, lol ☺ ☺ ☺ Sure you'll be feeling so much better once that vision clears up 👀 👍 👍

Bruce I love the way you inspire and explain the MM journey and the things you do to survive daily, with even mentioning your Amazon deliveries because of being housebound. Keep up the fight, warrior.

Ocean Dreams
January 16, 2020

Yabba Dabba Do !

It's Thursday evening!

Whelp, I fell asleep. I think??? Tuesday late afternoon, and since that afternoon I've been fast asleep and/or semi-awake but never nearly "awake."

It seems when I shift into "zombie," I sleep a few hours... da-da-DEEP sleep... dream, dream, dream. (Everly Brothers got nothin' on me.)

I suppose the reason I wake is my increasing interest in staying dry, but I dream of ocean waves crashing and a softly babbling brook. The end of the scene is a close up of a drip, drip... slower... slower...

Drip

Drip

In the dream... "rye chair" (rye chair is Cape Girardeau speak; translated: "Right there.")

So, In the dream... rye chair... I am tossed roughly into a wake place.

So I wake.

...grab Kane...

And I'm Chicago-style tottellin (you know, that "tot tell un" town)... totellin ... to the sand box??? (Recall, this is a dream, after all.)

I finish and return to either the recliner or the bed.

Two hours later the process is repeated, including the sand box part.

Then today "once my body has 'caught up' " I get to fully wake up. I'm caught up.

Why, if I'm so awake it's safe for me to drive, right??

Uh, not really... I'm dosed on Oxy... no vision in the left eye... blurred vision in the right eye (blurred vision, a pesky side effect of the drug I'm on... Belantamab Mafodotin... in a clinical trial. So who know what might happen to me out on the roads?

But this is Thursday, so I'll now start the fifth cycle of the trial drug.

No driving. Not safe. Order in from local grocery stores... local Chinese restaurants...

Amazon.

"Ellie dog, here comes the Amazon truck!!! Beggin' Strips!! Beggin' strips!! Next day delivery, Ellie!"

The UPS trunk just grunted 'round the cul-de-sac and is headed my way.

Now where's my smart phone... I need to order in my lunch delivery. Mexican today... double taco, mild sauce... 2 liter Coke... extra burrito to rewarm for dinner...

Done. Easy peasy.

And so it goes and so it goes.

Comments:

Got a copy of your first book!! Such an inspiration for me and all our Multiple Myeloma warriors! Thanks for sharing!

Sending daily prayers for stability and healing on your journey!

Journey Strong.

Ahhhh the ocean waves! So glad you have a smart phone to order Ellie's treats... and your dinner of course. AND NO, NO driving under the influence!! May your toes stay warm and your belly be full, my friend!!

Lucky you live in a metropolitan area where you have those options for meal delivery.

Bruce Morton What a beautiful way to minister to others!! I will be taking some copies with me both here in Columbus at the John B. Amos Cancer Center, and at Emory in Atlanta!

Flagged!

January 18, 2020

Flagged!

I've been flagged. And that's a GOOD thing.

I found out just yesterdee that my account with the hospital, Cancer Center and the docs is flagged, and that means... at least for now... a lower monthly payment.

About a month ago I had a "green color" statement PLUS a "red color" statement. Two statements and "they" were expecting two payments to be made by me each month. Fiddlesticks!

But as of now my red color statement and me has been "flagged."

Why wasn't I told? I would have celebrated... Payday candy bar....

The plan is for me to first pay down the green color account... pay it down all the way to nothing at the current monthly rate, and THEN "they" will come knockin' for the red account pay down.

Yep. I'm flagged.

Peanuts from my celebration Payday candy bar stuck in my teeth.

BTW, for as long as I've been on this MM journey I've applied for numerous assistance programs and co-pay grants. And we (me and caregiver Karen) have received approval most of the time. By far, most of the time "they" say "yes."

Our secrets to success? First APPLY EVERYWHERE... there's assistance money available, and all you have to do is apply.

But if you do get turned down... and this is our second secret to successful assistance approval... APPLY AGAIN if you initially are told, "No."

"No" is just a request for more information about your circumstances. Be polite. Fill in the gaps in information you've already provided.

Yep, you too will soon be "flagged."

And so it goes and so it goes

Comments:

> *I cannot imagine being in the US without Universal health care.*
>
> *Glad things are working out.*
>
> *I continue to try to explain to other Canadians why we need to guard this and improve it.*
>
> *Glad you are flagged!*

Happy Anniversary

January 19, 2020

Whelp, we missed it, folks.

"It" was on Friday, and I was very asleep most all day and night. (Lately, including Friday, Saturday, and today, my body is saying, "We're done" .... " OFF!!"... "pee, then head back to bed!!!")

So I missed " it "...

As we say in Cape Girardeau, I didn't pay it any nevermind.

Yep, missed it.

The anniversary of my dx of cancer.

I've completed seven years of treatment for Multiple Myeloma.

At the time of dx I was told that life expectancy was five to seven years. Gulp!

There are a ton of new treatment drugs and drug combos that weren't even around back in 2013.

So, up next? Whelp, right now I'm in a clinical trial for a new drug. When we put the wrap on that drug, I have to find a new solution for me; my hope is to find some other clinical trial that can use me to help bring their new MM solution drug to market. We need more of these treatment-type drugs as we wait for a true cure for MM.

For now, what's next is only :

> Happy Anniversary to me
>
> Happy Anniversary to me
>
> Happy Anniversary to the sick guy over there (Why, he don't look sick?!)
>
> Happy Anniversary to meeeeeee!

And so it goes , and so it goes

Comments:

> *Happy anniversary!*
>
> *Yep, this month is my nine year anniversary of diagnosis and treatment, in 2011, but had been extremely sick with what became known to me as Myeloma for over 4 months prior! At the time of diagnosis I was told life expectancy was 2 to 3 years! Now, 9 years later, I'm very, happily surprised at the number of new drugs available! Happy you're still here Bruce! Happy I'm still here! We need to, LIVE IN TO A CURE!*

Mike

January 20, 2020

So many of you prayed recently for my brother Mike. While in surgery for a quad bypass and a torn aorta, the aorta ruptured and in the vernacular, Mike "bled out." They say he was clinically dead for thirty-four minutes... he says there was a "very white light" while he was "out."

The docs said, "Step aside while we fix him," and they did. They are so wonderful, them docs.

Mike is out of ICU. I've spoken to him, and we are all encouraged that yes, he's gonna make it.

We all appreciate how fleeting life can be, and once we, or one close to us, has a brush with our mortality, things are just different in so many ways.

Celebrate each day as a special gift to us.

Smile and make others smile.

And so it goes and so it goes.

Comments:

That is great news!

So happy for his progress!

God is so good all the time.

Yet Another Specialist!

January 25, 2020

Well, coming up Thursday is an exciting day in MM-ville. I'll get to take out my MM journey specialist PUNCH CARD and stab out the ORAL SURGEON location.

Yep, yep - Thursday I'll see about these mouth sores, which they tell me will be treated with surgery or maybe just medication

So... another specialist brought on to my care team... oral surgeon. Oh boy!

I'll report back what they call what these sores are... fortunately not really sore... just not right, and sensitive to heat which is seriously getting in the way of me enjoying dem Dominos late nite hot chicken wings...

The oral surgeon doc will fix me up.

"You'll be fine, Mr Morgan."

And so it goes and so it goes.

Comments:

> *Do we have any parts that can't be touched by MM? I don't think so. Good luck!* 🖤

Laughter Infection

January 29, 2020

"Wha you chucklin' 'bout?" came a pleasant voice.

I was in getting my hair cut.

"Can you hear that? " I asked.

"Yeah. Wha you chucklin' 'bout? I wants to know so I'll chuckle too."

Then comes a shriek of a laugh we both enjoyed, me and the hair dresser person.

"I'm cuttin' har and you chucklin'. What up with that?"

Truth be told I do chuckle along the way throughout my day. Sorta bird-chirpy cluck actually.

I chuckle when I've nothing much to chuckle about but this har cutter person was the first to ever hear my warble.

"I chuckle a lot because I'm happy a lot. You heard me, eh?"

"Oh yeah, I heard you. I don't chuckle, I HOOT!"

Then what wafted from her, I swear, rattled the conditioner shelf.

Then we both laughed again.

Loud laugh.

And why not? Laughing is infectious, eh?

Laughing is the one infectious thing I can stand to be around without getting sick from it.

So, that's my muse on laughing my way through this MM journey.

Laugh loud enough for others to hear me, yeah. Not just my happy warble. A full bore laugh.

Not just a smile ... not just a chuckle that nobody hears.

Nope... laugh!

Make 'em ask, "What's he laughing about??? I thought he had cancer."

And so it goes and so it goes.

Comments:

> As I'm reading, I'm imagining the laughter and laughing, too. 😄😄😄 Sometimes it's only laughter that gets us through a tough day. It will definitely help us along the myeloma journey.

> Bruce, I'm laughing with tears of joy reading this! You bring out the best in people, and make them wonder why you're so happy. 😃 Happy to be here, that's why.

You always know how to make us laugh.

I have a picture that says, "Take time to laugh; it is the music of the soul." Thank you for sharing and making me smile and chuckle ☺☺

Laughter can cure a lot, even if it's for a short time... keep it up, Bruce. ☺☺☺

I need to laugh more-thanks for the reminder. :). My 3 year old granddaughter is coming over soon for me to watch-she will help me with that. :)

My husband makes me laugh all the time. It's great. ☺♥☺

I love this. I love reading the funny thoughts on FB. My day doesn't really begin until I read Dennis, Baby Blues, Mutts, etc. Get the good feelings started.

They say laughter is the best medicine. That's because the copay is $0. Keep fighting the good fight.

Laughing is my hero when needed. Great post.

Bruce thanks for the laugh. I need to laugh much more and you are the person who reminds me!

Side Effects

February 4, 2020

Right now this MM journey is a struggle. Whew, a struggle in so many ways. It's high time to face off against those places where the MM has "position" on me, and at very least hold my ground and do my best to push back at the MM. A noticeable "push back" is what needs to happen.

I've let the neuropathy in my feet "run" for a bit. In the trial I'm in we need to discover how the new drug combos with old drug Velcade, which in the past has given me neuropathy in my feet.

Ouch! Double Ouch!!

The doc reduced the Velcade dose, but still this neuropathy is doing me in. (Did I mention the Ouch part?)

Lay in more Gabapentin. Fooey. Still no relief.

So we'll see what the doc and the trial sponsors say to do. Maybe drop the Velcade altogether?

Next on the list... a new frontier for me: mouth sores. I've been lucky, and 'til now on this MM journey I've not been visited by sores in my mouth.

Now I have some.

Yup, now I have 'thsome.'

Ouch! Double Ouch!!

Does this new trial drug produce painful mouth thsores? Whelp, in me it thsure, by cracky, has.

So I slosh with Majic Mouthwash, a prescription from the doc that's got Benadryl and Lanacane and a secret ingredient to make it taste extra foul. Orajel on the most hurty places helps a bit.

There's also the issue of blurred vision. We have changed eye drops, and that's been better in the last week or so. I think I could drive now.

Lastly is the fatigue that moves in and sets up a home for three days at a time. Knocks me FLAT. Then I might have one day where I'm up and walking around a bit... then the fatigue comes back, and I'm down and out for three days again. Whew!

So... at least in me this new trial drug means neuropathy in the feet... mouth sores... blurred vision and fatigue. Oh boy!

But, hey buddy, it seems that the stuff DOES work to push back at the MM. When we started the trial my Lambda Light Chains number was 100 or so; currently that number is just 9! That's VERY low for me.

The trial continues. We learn a little bit each day about this new drug.

And so it goes and so it goes.

Comments:

LIVE IN TO A CURE!

Sending you light, love and strength to keep up the fight.

I got neuropathy from Velcade too. Gabapentin never helped. The only thing I have found to ease it is hydrocodone (which sucks to use a narcotic) and CBD cream rubbed on my feet from the health food store. Hope you find some relief from it too.

I recently read where Dana Farber gives IV saline to their patients on their Velcade days which seems to lessen the neuropathy... something to consider? No idea how much, etc., but perhaps your MM doc can reach out to his DFCI colleagues and inquire.

I got desperate one night and put vapor rub on mine. The menthol did help some with my feet. My sinuses were great!

Again With the Side Effects
February 13, 2020

Trial update and ALL of it is good!

Uh, well MOST of its good!

Uh, well THE IMPORTANT STUFF AT LEAST IS GOOD.

Uh, well SOME OF THE STUFF IS LIKE, SORTA GOOD...

Hey lookie here, I learned a long time ago not to try and balance the good against the bad in my MM journey.

Each day we are allowed is a gift, eh?

The trial I'm in, it appears, will result in a new MM treatment brought to market as a single agent to push back on our MM. And, it's in a new class of drugs, so it will be worth a go for many of us as we wait for that elusive MM cure.

The trial I'm in shows this drug brings with it a few pesky side effects. However, I'd say the side effects were minor and well "worth it."

I'd like to be on this drug for a good long while.

Yippee!

Now, unrelated to the trial drug I have a new travel companion:

Mouth sores. (Same ones as the previous entry…)

Phooey!

I'm told the sores come about cuz of the Zometa I took in the past, and are called *osteonecrosis*, which may be a useful word if you are losing at Scrabble… but I'll need to punch back at these guys before I have any affection for them. They HURT.

There's a super sauce mouthwash known as "Magic Wash" or by some as "Swish and Spit," I think. They combine Lanacane and Benadryl, and just the right amount of foul taste to make a prescription swisheroo that makes me wonder in Peggy Lee style, "Is that all there is," cuz this mouth swish stuff isn't much of a mouth sore solution.

I dab a bit of Orajel on each sore place and that helps a bit. I'm told these things don't heal

Double Phooey.

And so it goes and so it goes

Comments:

Ugh. So freaking sorry! (about the mouth sores)

YIPPIE! (about the meds!)

Hang in there, Bruce Morton!

Spread Love!

February 13, 2020

Okay, tomorrow is Valentine's Day and it's traditional for me to not spend any time lamenting Valentine's greetings not received, but instead to do my best to spread as many "I love you " greetings as I can.

It's easy and fun. Works with a phone call to mom who is 94 years young, or to others who are young I may just send a text or Facebook PM.

"Hi _____. It's Bruce. Today is Valentine's Day and I love YOU."

Then I just shut up. We chat for a bit, and then I move on to the next person on my "love list."

Give it a try. It's fun. And it sure beats waiting around for somebody to say "I love you" to me!

And so it goes and so it goes

Comments:

> *I love this idea.*
>
> ♥ *What a wonderful idea. Happy Valentine's Day, Bruce Morton.* ✉

Did I Mention Side Effects?

February 24, 2020

Well, I've been absent here for a bit as I try to accommodate my new travel companion on this MM journey.

Mr. Neuropathy hops on board overnight, so I wake up with pain at a "10," and it's from there I try to get some relief. Right now, the systemic combo of Oxy and Gabapentin doubled up has finally brought relief and I'm ready to get out my pogo stick.

Not really.

The back story; I signed up to be in a clinical trial that included the drug Velcade, which most of us have taken I suppose. I don't do well on Velcade. My platelet count shot to the floor. And then there's this neuropathy…

Ooops.

So I've been given a string of platelet transfusions, and we stopped further dosing of the Velcade.

Now, on to a "fix" for the neuropathy in the feets.

We'll figure it out, and then I can get to the pesky mouth sores and blurred vision.

And I'll get an MRI March 7 to chase down the pain in my spine. That, I'm guessing, is a return of the tumor from last summer.

Double Ooops.

(Hee hee if I could juuuust dig my way out from under the deep fatigue that sits on me most days, I'd be better at going at all this.)

I'm encouraged that these MM issues... at least to some extent... are all treatable. My dog Ellie and I can still play until we tire and need to take a comforting rest.

Comforting rest.

A good nap.

My appetite is good, and that BBQ chicken Mac and Provel cheese is callin' my name for lunch today. (Provel cheese is ONLY available here in St. Louis I'm told, so that's a special treat...)

And so it goes and so it goes.

Comments:

> *At least neuropathy from Velcade is more reversible than others. Hope it reverses soon.*

> *Bruce my Bruce! You never disappoint us with your stories! ☺ Praying they get you right this time, and that the neuropathy gets better.*

As They Say in "The Cape"

February 29, 2020

Ha! Not sure why this comes to mind but the thought seemed to help me.

I'm from Jackson, Missouri just outside Cape Girardeau... Cape... Missouri, where language and local phrases have been perfected, and I miss not living there to soak some of that in from time to time.

For one example, "Here currently" simply means "now," just with bit more of the person speaking invested into it.

"How are you?" Is asked; the "here currently" added to the response pulls the listener in... "Here currently there's this neuropathy."

"Here currently" can be unnerving. Living in the "now" is truly so often our only choice.

"Here currently" my feet HURT! Where's that Australian roll on goop!?"

But "Here currently" is not my only choice, and right out of Jackson, Missouri I'm gifted with the phase...

"Here directly."

I'll complete the phase my way: "Here directly something WONDERFUL will happen in my life."

Over-the-top WONDERFUL, Here directly.

We learn stuff every extra moment we are allowed to stay here another day. We learn that if that "living in the present" just ain't cuttin' it, then we can know and consider that "Here directly something WONDERFUL is goin' to happen."

Stay ever hopeful of wonderful that is just around the corner... Here directly.

(Hee hee... thanks for the language lesson, my Uncle Merrill... I miss you..."

And so it goes and so it goes

Comments:

Stay positive, Brother Bruce.

I miss my mom's "Missouri Speak".... 🖤🖤🖤

Thank for the laugh. Feeling crappy tonight. Laughs are appreciated.

Bruce, I lived in Cape for 20 years and loved it. That is one reason I love to read your writing. May God bless you with a lot less pain.

Very Interesting!

Life Is the Bubbles

March 1, 2020

No picture, but here's my "it helped with my neuropathy" tip of the week.

Dirty dishes had piled in the sink.

I knew I'd be there for a while, so I stood barefoot on bubble wrap envelopes fresh from Amazon.

Actually made standing much nicer

Ahhhhhhh...

And so it goes and so it goes.

Comments:

> There are days when I want to chop off my feet and hands...
>
> It is tough when the cramps and charlie horses are so bad you want to just dx cream.
>
> I had purchased a bubble bathmat - should have been the most comfy thing ever... I thought I was standing on stones! I can't tell you how many times I picked it up, thinking the dogs dragged in a stone pile.
>
> Is it as fun to pop with your toes as it is by hand? 😊 Seriously, if it works, don't knock it, right?

Pain!

March 11, 2020

Karen drove me to the ER on Monday morning 10:00a.m.

Severe pain in my back.

Yep we are talking *severe*. I put Ellie into the back yard and I went back inside to scream out in pain... several times.

I thought for certain it was a revisit to the Stone Age... the Kidney Stone Age.

But no. CT was clear.

Hours later and no letup in the pain. Let's dose Bruce wif more pain killer. After the morphine we go to Fentanyl.

No relief. So out comes the Toradol.

Nope. Still no relief. It's hour six. So we spin the wheel, and it stops at Dilaudid.

You guessed it... Still hurts just as bad as the previous seven hours.

The service in the ER has gone from bad to bah-bah-bad-awful.

No food or drink, and the talk is I'll soon be moved to "Big Barnes," which is local-speak for the largest hospital in St. Louis; the one that that handles all the gunshot trauma in the city, which is our number three industry just behind car theft and knife wounds.

The wait time is minimum six hours there, and the neighborhood is questionable in the daytime and downright for sure dangerous at night.

And there are no available beds at Big Barnes. Did I mention the gunshot wounds they handle each day? I'd surely be in line behind all the action crimes victims.

After ten and a half hours of waiting, opioid dosing and no food or drink, word of an available room soon is rumored; so the decision is made to ship me to Big Barnes, where the chairs in the waiting room are more stained and much more uncomfortable.

However, just up the street is where my MM specialist offices are, and there are PLENTY of opioids in the surrounding neighborhood.

It's hour eleven now and I can drink and eat and wait and hurt better at Big Barnes... or so I'm told.

We try oxycodone. Finally some relief!

Right now it's Wednesday.

After a series of tests on Tuesday: MRI, CT, X-ray, Blood labs, etc....

We know nothing.

However I can eat, drink, wait, and I hurt a bit less.

Not much let up in the pain in my back...
Tomorrow more tests.

And so it goes and so it goes.

Comments:

> *Coronavirus fears are clogging our ERs*
>
> *Oh, oh, I so wish I could relieve your pain. In my Myeloma experience, pain has been the worst of it! Numerous times I have had to endure severe, debilitating pain! Pain is what would lead me to the edge, and possibly step over! Anyway, will keep my heart and spirit on your bucket's edge, to help you cope, until you hopefully get a conclusion to this pain episode. You have survived so very much Myeloma crap. This, too, shall pass... at some point... most definitely sooner! My existence only occurs with enough Oxycodone and Fentanyl. Stick it out, demand and find a solution. As all of us MM sufferers (whoops, survivors) know, Quality of Life is everything! Hopefully we will, LIVE IN TO A CURE!*
>
> *You know something is wrong, even if they haven't found anything yet...we know what our horrid bone pain is - when I was diagnosed it came*

going down my spine and right hip. My back was broken more than once, then my hip. Keep on it - your pain is never imagined!

Mine was a tumor inside my t10 vertebrae pushing against my spinal cord... then radiation treatments added to the pain but now much better! Hope you get some answers ASAP!!

God Bless you, Bruce. I am so sorry. I pray your pain has subsided. I have SMM and Arthritis real bad. I have had a hip replacement. That helped that problem, but there is always something to begin to hurt. I am 85 and tired of pain. Hope you are better today.

St. Jude Children's Research Hospital

ALSAC • Danny Thomas, Founder

Finding cures. Saving children.

Oops... Quarantine
March 19, 2020

Hello, MM lads and lassies.

All is well here, but I'm stuck here in hospital because they can't release an immunity-reduced person into Corona risk.

Pain will get solved... I have a GREAT MM TEAM! PRAY FOR THEM.

Comments:

> Good to hear from you Bruce! I pray for your team and all other medical staff on the front lines. This too shall pass, but praying for sooner so you can go home to your baby girl!

> Bruce Morton you're a hoot and my favorite... perhaps also because my family is from Creve Coeur and surrounding areas.

> Prayers for you Bruce 🙏 Glad to see a post hoping things continue to improve. Thinking of you ♥

Maybe Tomorrow

March 19, 2020

I'm pointed towards home 😃. Released tomorrow, if neuropathy is like a 3 or lower. Neuropathy lowering meds are already in my pie hole. Yay! And yay!!!

We can ratchet up neuropathy meds to speed up response. Yay and double yay 😃😃😃

I can get Ellie dog out of kennel boarding.

Next post could be from home. 😃😃😃 I'm managing my expectations, and a few things need to happen to truly get me released.

Lots and lots of wonderful new knowledge I look forward to sharing with y'all.

And so it goes and so it goes.

Comments:

Woohoo! That's such wonderful news! 💔

Yay! Hope it all works out!

I'm Back!

March 19, 2020

Hey Partners' Group... a special shout out to my "gul fran" here at the Partners' Group for helping me recall how to post to private groups. I had not posted for like 11 days, and I went brain dead... and so I messaged her for help, and we got 'er done 😁

Comments:

Welcome back, Bruce!!! 💗💗💗

Goin' Home... NOT

March 20, 2020

Oops, I thought I was discharged from this hospital but, alas, no. I met all the health requirements for discharge 'cept for one. In my best Maxwell Smart: missed it by THAT much...

I'm stuck here until a home health nurse is found to train me for an IV antibiotic regimen. You know: "Here's how you hang the bag of antibiotic, Mr. Morgan." Apparently the one trainer in St Louis is unavailable until Sunday... something about a pandemic???

So, I'll be Gilbert Gottfried, and be UP ALL NIGHT on DEX here in the hospital for day #12... Facebook Message me at 2:00 a.m. to chat. ☺

Discharge on Sunday is ????

Poor Ellie. ☹

And so it goes and so it goes.

Comments:

>   May you and Ellie be reunited very soon!! She's so sweet looking. ♥♥

FINALLY Home Again!

March 21, 2020

I am home. I had to break out of the hospital by eating my cheeseburger as I walked slowly past the nurses' station.

"Where are you going, Mr. Morgan?"

Punch "Lobby" and OUT. The front door. Ha!

Family was NOT happy with me as they wanted me CLOSER to all the incoming COVID-19 that's in the hospital. ☺

I invited them to take my now empty bed on the 10th floor. So far no takers... hmmmmm.

St. Louis is under full lockdown, and I chose to ride this out with just me and dog, Ellie.

And so it goes and so it goes

Comments:

Awesome that you're home! Please take care of yourself. 👪 ❤

Take care. I sure don't blame you.

Be safe and stay in touch with us!

I hope that means you're home and safe.

The Real Heroes
March 21, 2020

Lil' more about my hospital stay...

I'm home now.

I learned a new way to express our delight with a series of blood counts that replaces the fist bump "perfect..." Remember, no touching or hand shaking now in this new COVID-19 world... Do a thumbs up 👍 and smile BIG and say, "Golden!"

I met Corey in the waiting room outside radiation; Corey is just now fifteen months old and he was crying; but only a bit; coming out of treatment eight to his tiny brain. Folks, imagine that scene.

Note to self: How can my little bout of diarrhea be compared to Corey's brain radiation treatment - #8?

Or the nurse I met whose boy is a cancer survivor... she worked her way through nursing school... 20 years at Walmart... dedicating her life now to being a cancer nurse.

Folks, I'm no "Warrior" compared to her... least not in my mind.

I have two new and EXCITING MM project ideas here now as my MM progresses... AND it's time for our next book to compile for Amazon Publishing.

Ellie and I are reunited, and if you're a dog person you "get" that.

And so it goes and so it goes.

Comments:

> *Bruce - so good to hear from you. So happy that you and Ellie are both home. Sorry, but you are a warrior. Don't short-change yourself. You have been through quite a lot, and everyone is praying things will turn around for you. Looking forward to another book!!* ♣ 🙉

> *Been hoping to see your next edition of Cancer Bows to a Smile, yay! Congrats on getting home, and prayers always for others who suffer more.* ♥

From Bruce:

It's September 2020… Our book #2 should go to publishing by the end of this month.

And Back We Go

March 25, 2020

I'm back in the hospital. Whew.

Out then back in. No symptoms of virus. Then chest X-ray, then swab, and no detectable evidence of virus. That swab test hurts... they will test me again, I'm sure.

I'm NOT sure of ANYTHING else. After my bold breakout of 2020, I went in to a major level of Dex Day confusion that culminated in me turning myself in to the local police on the parking lot of the local grocery. Ambulance took me to ER, where I was then admitted back into the hospital. That was Monday morning, 7 a.m.

Pray hard for me. My plight is a combo mix of DEX... confusion, and the MM... and all the fear of COVID means no one is available to be discharged to go home.

For about 10 hours, dog Ellie was loose with no collar, but she is secured now.

And so it goes and so it goes.

Comments:

God is good all the time!

Bruce Morton very interesting post. I went on a drug high on the same day I took Dex and Selinexor. I could have floated to the ceiling and met my wife up there!!!!! I had a ball of a time.

I'd be interested to know if you or any of the other warriors here have had similar experiences. ☺

I've had a multitude of strange occurrences. I've been getting confused. And incoherent at times. Like I'm taking to someone and then I'm talking about something different with no bridge. Like extreme ADHD. A few times I've felt VERY high, like pain meds were amplified. I've taken steroids off and on for three decades, and I don't remember ever having the issues I've had this month. And I'm on reduced dose 20 mg.

Bruce, you asked that we pray hard for you and I will. I ask that God wraps his arm around you with blessings and guidance as you go through this rough period. He will always give you what you need when you need it.

8 mg/wk of Dex is working for me. I will take it tonight at bedtime. I pray they get you stabilized, Brother Bruce.

Where to Go?

March 27, 2020

A while ago they took away my sitter and put me back in my street clothes, and I'm told I'm no longer considered an elopement risk.

Problem for the hospital is: where do we discharge Bruce to?

I'm not much help answering that question, as my four family members here in St. Louis have made the right smart decision to not take part in any way in said discharge.

My long list of friends, the same thing: "Hospital, keep him!"

Except for two dear and bold friends who won't stay with me, but will be there as I gain access to my house. Just two, alas.

And so it goes and so it goes.

Comments:

> *Hoping a temporary resting stop is found for you ASAP. Best of everything to you!*
>
> *Maybe it's time to buy the house and start our own MM reality show.* 😊

Home Again, for Now

April 3, 2020

I am home from the hospital at last!

Admitted on March 9 with what turned out to be a couple of pesky tumors on my back. Those boys got ten radiation treatments. Pow!

Way too much neuropathy in my feet, so the good doctors started playing "take away" and "here, try this" with my Gabapentin and Oxy.

"Here comes Mr. Morphine!!!"

Bottom line is that all that mucking with my meds... and introducing a multitude of new meds... completely set me adrift.

I'll share the highlights and lowlights of my three week adventure that included me busting out of the hospital (that's called an 'elopement') without a time wasting formal "discharge." Oh yes, and I got to meet my local police patrol... TWICE!!! "Is there a problem, officer???"

I will have a telecom with my MM team on Tuesday.

Praise God for seeing me through.

And so it goes and so it goes.

Comments:

> Bruce, what are we going to do with you??? 😕 Tumors need to schedule an appointment with you, and you need to cancel every time. Now you know you can't just leave the hospital. I hope you had on clothes and not just the hospital gown. Well, glad to hear you are home now where Ellie can keep an eye on you. 😁😁 Take care my friend.

> Ditto the "Praise God" part!

> So glad you are safe at home. The hospital isn't fun. Wishing we could go to a concert together. Maybe The Beatles? Or Streisand in her day? Open to suggestions. Take care, Bruce. 🖤

> Soooooooo wonderful to hear from you!! Glad that you still have your sense of humor.

> Good to read of your escapades, all is right with the world. Well, besides this whole pandemic thing. 😀 ✌ 🙏 💓

> We have all missed reading your posts. So happy you are home. You and Ellie can take care of each other.

> Stay strong, Brother Bruce!

> I can understand why ANYONE would make a decision to "BUST OUT" of a hospital... ANY hospital!

"The Rest of the Story"
April 5, 2020

I'll give a quick recap of my hospital stay in March. On March 9 mid-morning I presented with a piercing pain reminiscent of a kidney stone I'd met up with in 2017. I first called my caregiver sister Karen who lives about 40 miles away in Illinois.

If we are counting, that was mistake #1, because my pain level shot up out of sight.

I should have called 911. I waited for Karen And waited. And waited.

I later was to learn that after seven years of rushing to my aid no matter what time of day, Karen had understandably reached her limit.

We rushed to ER, and now my pain is a 10. They quick give me a CT Scan. There wasn't a kidney stone. And they thankfully started upping my pain meds: Oxycodone, Fentanyl, Dilaudid, Morphine…

That there was the beginning of a three week journey that included BIG doses of pain meds mixed with antidepressants like Lexapro and Zyprexa, plus antianxiety drugs.

Now, three weeks later, most of the drugs are still in me. I can FEEL them in me.

After that first Monday I was still in a LOT of pain... back pain, and now the neuropathy in my feet got away from us.

Mistake #2: I totally underestimated how neuropathy pain can completely take over. It... at least for me... is unrelenting and the only thing to be done is to find the right pain med and increase the dose to get some relief.

They found a couple of lesions on my back around the pain area and scheduled me for 10 radiation treatments.

And Oxycodone for my neuropathy... 15mg I think.

Finally some pain relief, but my March Ordeal was just beginning. All my med doses were modified, and most of the drugs I was taking before March 9 were mucked with... Gabapentin, Oxycodone , OxyContin, Morphine, our old friend Dexamethasone, Lexapro, Zyprexa, Ativan, Benadryl, and a whole host of antibiotics.

By late in that first week I was a jumble of harsh drugs interacting with each other.

I'll say it... I went "nuts." There's a name for it "Hospital delirium." Google it.

HD is not your ordinary "confusion," or having a bad Dex day. It takes two hands to count the number of times I urinated myself wet. I was tethered to a "bed alarm" to restrain me from wandering off.

Early on in the March Madness journey, sister Karen was there for me but my behavior got really bizarre. I was constantly flunking the "confusion" questions. I had no idea where I was, or what year it was.

By about the fifth day of chaos and bad behavior, Karen was rightly fed up with me and we began to differ... arguing what the right course of action should be. We fussed. Frustration.

Finally a really, really good doc happened upon this mayhem and rightly concluded "we've got you all messed up" and he chopped in to the too-long list of my meds. That helped, but still the "balance" of all those drugs wasn't right.

I wasn't "right."

That's not Bruce.

I had two weeks yet to go in the hospital. At one point, I was so afraid I "eloped" on Saturday, which is when you just up and leave the hospital, not having been formally discharged. That's never a good idea, and in my case the local police were waiting for me in front of my house. I'd committed no crime and the hospital was just worried for my safety.

I wasn't "right."

That's not Bruce.

When I "eloped," I left all my meds in my room, so I was in desperate need of some Oxy for my feet.

I plunged myself into my predicament, my head pounding from the confusion.

That Sunday is a blur. Early on I called Karen and she explained that she was "caregivered" out, and she and her family agreed that she needed to be hands-off caregiver duties. That was no surprise as my behavior of late was pretty awful.

That's not Bruce!

Later on that Sunday night, the delirium really hit. I got myself locked out of my house. At first Ellie was with me. Complete delirious state. I could not think. Demons were coming down the street after me. I was cold, very cold. I'd peed myself wet several times. I was locked out of my house and to get back in, I hurled a jackstand through my barely living living room window. I have the pictures.

That's not Bruce!

I just wanted the police to come rescue me.

Finally at first light... this was the first Monday of the lockout out here in St. Louis... I hooked up with police. But Ellie was loose with no collar.

The police called EMS, and before long I was back in the same hospital room I had eloped from.

Alone with no caregiver. The hospital needed a responsible family member, and I had none. This is where COVID-19 prevented my kids or well-meaning friends from helping me.

After eight more days in the hospital, and aided by the encouragement and prayers of local friends, I was close to being "right."

But still no caregiver... and the hospital would not discharge me unless I had one. No way, no how, after my elopement were they taking any chances. I'm now forever a "flight risk."

Praise God, I found a home health care company that would satisfy the hospital requirements.

Ellie was found, confused yet safe.

I'm home and I now wear a Life Alert button 24/7.

And so it goes and so it goes

Comments:

Oh Bruce, I'm so sorry. Karen will be back, just give her time. I'm glad to know you are okay. Life Alert is closer than Karen anyway. I know she loves you. You hang in there, you keep me going, especially in these crazy days♥ ♥ .

Bruce, sorry you had to go through all of this. I'm glad your meds sound sorted out and corrected for you. I hope it stays that way. I agree that your sister, Karen, will be back. This COVID-19 has everyone on edge. She will be there for you. Stay safe! 🙏🙏🙏

Oh my, Bruce! That is quite the ordeal. Hugs!!

So very glad you have been "found!" Wonderful that you can still maintain any amount of your darkly delightful humor through all this! What an adventure, for good or bad, better or worse! When your head clears more, we hope, write your nightmare of an adventure down, remembering what you can, adding more over time as recollections come back. Well, life marches on, amazingly quickly, with or without us! Be careful! Be sure to design some safety and caretaking of yourself, by others! Our minds! They sure can vacate at times! I am rambling myself! Hope, very much, that you are continuing to improve. Wish you had more family checking in and watching you! But, I have absolutely none, so understand! Take care. Be safe! Be resilient! Just be first! Want to hear from you soon!

Bruce, I'm so sorry for all you have endured. I understand your sister's need for a break from caregiving, but I feel angry and sad that you are alone. Praying for better days ahead for you.

Getting Back on the Pony
April 8, 2020

I am discovering more and more each and every day of my MM journey.

I spent three weeks in the hospital this time around; three ambulance rides; two CT scans; three MRIs; the equivalent of three full body x-rays; ten radiation treatments to two new tumors on my back. Add five new drugs, and take away or reduce dosage of four drugs. At least three, and possibly four, episodes of deep confusion... I failed those "Where are you, Mr. Morton" tests. I busted out of the hospital without a formal hospital discharge. On two separate occasions, local police got involved. "First name..." (BTW, the police were great!!! I can truly say they saved my life when they got me safely into the arms of the first responders.)

Now I can rest. I was thrown off the pony HARD.

Rest? Nah, I want get back up on that clinical trial pony and use my body to help bring this new drug to market.

Now it is time to get my skinny white butt back on that clinical trial pony... pick up where I fell off.

Yesterday at the Cancer Center, we started getting me active in the trial. But oops, my platelet count sucks... just 20, and I need that to be a minimum 25.

So they gave me a transfusion of platelets, and platelets are hard to come by... nobody is donating blood and platelets. And after transfusion, my platelet count got a whopping... Ready for it... 24.

"Go home, Mr. Morton."

I go in again on Friday to try and get my platelet count up to 25.

Folks we need this new drug as an additional drug to call up when we become refractory to other therapies. The trial is open and looking for new participants. Come on, folks, the only way to kick back at MM is to pick ourselves up and reenter the dance with MM.

Hopefully on Friday my platelets will have recovered, and they will start me up with the trial.

And so it goes and so it goes.

Comments:

Re-enter the dance with MM. I love this!

-I did this myself yesterday after staying home without treatment for 2wks (against my drs opinion). Sheer panic. So I went back with extra

stamina. I'm compulsively safe... mask and gloves. Strip down and showered when I got back. It actually felt strengthening!

Thank you for your words this morning—and come on platelets! You've got this! 💪

Thank you Bruce for fighting for us all.

You give me a smile and great hope with each of your posts! You are a humorous warrior!!

When I was dx 2-1/2 years ago my specialist said, "This cancer is not curable but it IS treatable!" I was thinking, you know, a little chemo and take a pill. Nooooooo. I have learned "treatable" can be very serious!

What a crazy time you have been having. You can't make this stuff up! So glad you're doing better, home and with Ellie. Praying your platelets come up a little. Thank you so much for all you do for the other Multiple Myeloma warriors. We could not make it without you! Hang tough, Bruce.

25 on Friday? On it.

Praying for Platelets

April 9, 2020

Hi, everyone. I have a prayer request for me, but really it's for all of us. On Tuesday, even after a transfusion, I did not have enough platelets to get infused with the study drug. Trial participants need 25 platelets, and my count was only 24. Drat! Missed it by just one. "Go home Mr. Morgan... come back on Friday and we will try again."

Folks, I don't know how many tries I get but it would all be hunky-dory if my blood lab tomorrow is 25 or higher.

And if I can keep on getting treated with the study drug, that is good for all of us. It helps bring this new drug to market. But for me to help the study sponsors develop this drug, it's important that I continue in the trial.

So tomorrow, can you pray that my platelet count is at least 25?

Tomorrow evening I'll report back.

And so it goes, and so it goes.

Comments:

I love you! Sending love and prayers! 🙏 🙏 🙏

Come on, 25!!!! You can do it!

Bruce, prayer for the 25+. Sending love and big hugs to you. We will be waiting tomorrow to hear from you, buddy.

Belated prayers for ya, as I sure know what it's like to be watching those counts... for me the culprits are the absolute neutrophil counts... low counts have stopped me from doing chemo at least 3 to 4 times... Grrrrrr, oh well and all the best to ya!!!

Praying for you daily Bruce. Looking forward to good news on your platelets!

Praying 4 U, Bruce.

Platelets and a Picture
April 10, 2020

Praise God from whom all blessings flow!!

Folks, we did it!!! Thanks to all your prayers, my platelet count was juuuuuuust barely enough. I needed it to be 25, but on Tuesday 24 was the best I could do.

And today we got to 25, and that means I can start another cycle of the study drug. That's the green mystery bag containing the GSK clinical trial drug, and the happy happy guy in the red hat is me.

Again, thank you thank you for all the prayers sent up by you for me.

Happy Easter -

He is Risen!

And so it goes and so it goes.

Comments:

Woohoo! Hallelujah! Praise the Lord! 25 is such a great number.

Thank God, He is great! Continued prayers.

HALLELUJAH! Prayer works & God is STILL in the business of miracles!

The Lord is risen, indeed. There is HOPE!

Praise the Lord!! ❤

Glory to God!

Hallelujah.

Easter

April 12, 2020

Happy Easter to everyone!

He is risen!

Comments:

He is risen indeed!

Happy Easter 😊

To all my Multiple Myeloma Families. Be blessed today.

He is risen indeed! And praise God for his Mercy!

Show Us Your Pets

April 13, 2020

Ok I've not held an official "show us your pet" day for quite some time, so here we go, all you quarantined MM travelers!

Show everyone your pet. Everybody knows Ellie:

Show Us Your Wheels

April 20, 2020

Not long we showed off our fav pet, and that was quite a success. Now it's time to show off your fav ride. A restored vintage car or a brand new hot Mustang that you are proud of... the car that gets you a thumbs up as you speed by.

Here's my other British sports car, a restored 1971 MG Midget:

And so it goes, and so it goes.

Comments:

> I've driven and ridden in several exotic cars because my husband worked for a dealer, and then became a dealer. Favorite because of the way it took curves and rode is the Maserati. No pix. Just normal everyday life.

My husband and I have been binge watching "Comedians In Cars Getting Coffee." Great fun admiring the classic cars that are featured in each episode—and some of the comedians had us laughing so hard, we completely forgot why we were sheltered! 😊

My 1986 Buick Grand National

Ooh, and my favorite MG green color. Does it have a wooden steering wheel?

1970 280 SL.

1994 Corvette Coupe.

Bought this rusted MG to keep my mind off my MM. Did the body work and repainted it. Too bad the C-virus keeps me from driving it around. Stay safe, warriors.

My bike which I've had for over 12 years, but sadly my strength is too weak to hold her up.

See, I Told You It Would Heal!
April 28, 2020

I haven't posted to any of the Myeloma groups for quite a while.

I've been waiting. Waiting for some really good news I could report, and I'll admit I was being far too discerning... waiting for some really REALLY GREAT news.

And I got nuttin'.

Until today... I can report a really nice bit of news. Ya see, about two months ago I had these really bothersome mouth sores erupt... one on the lower left and one on the lower right. "Mr. Bruce, those are the result of the Zometa infusions, and those will never heal."

To which I answered "My name is Mr. Morton, and I'll put forth some prayers at dem sores and we'll just see if we can heal 'em up."

Sure enough, today a chunk of Bruce's jaw bone jimmied loose into my morning cheese grits and one of the two sores... had completely healed, and I'm pain free. Ha! One more to go.

There's a lesson in this of course, and that is not be too quick to believe the doom and gloom "it won't ever heal "prognosis we might hear from our medical team.

My medical team is the absolute BEST, but I'll put my money on my PRAYER TEAM every time.

Next up I'll focus on the pesky neuropathy in my feet. It's gonna take us a long time to try out all the possible drugs we can throw at that ailment.

My job is to take each ailment one by one.

As we are constantly told, each of us is different, so perhaps the solution to my neuropathy will be as individual and unique as me.

I'm just praying that the "fix" for my neuropathy doesn't turn out to be acupuncture! Yikes! Ouch!

"Hold still Mr. Bruce!!"

And so it goes and so it goes

Comments:

God is our healer! I am so glad you finally had some good news. Prayer is our answer.

Praise God for everything he has done for you!

You are truly an individual in a million and loaded with good spirits. Prayer never fails; just sometimes we don't understand the answers we get. Glad you got good ones and more coming, Mr. Bruce. ♥

Changes, Maybe

April 29, 2020

Well. It seems my MM specialist is suggesting a new drug for me to get to know in the near future:

Selinexor.

Can anyone tell me your experience with Selinexor? Was it in combo with other meds? Dexamethasone? Were there side effects?

I am clinging by my fingernails to stay in the clinical trial I've been in since November 2019. I expect that the dose I'll get on Tuesday will be my last... More news to follow on that. It's all good... just that there's a basket full of changes coming my way, because all my markers and blood counts have gone whacko on me... Alas.

A PET scan on Monday will reveal where we embark on this next leg of my MM journey. There is a tumor on my sternum that I'd affectionately named "Lumpy" that's grown considerably in the past month, and now will get radiation treatments... zap, zap.

And so it goes and so it goes.

Comments:

Stay strong. I was on Revlimid, Velcade and Dex. And I got 11 radiation treatments. Everyone's journey is different. I hope you beat it.

Good luck with the new treatment. You are on the cutting edge! ❤

Hey Bruce, ask your doctor about unexpected blackouts. It doesn't happen to everyone, but it is a known side effect. But it is a very effective drug in the few people I have heard of using it.

Bruce, I have been on Selinexor since June of 2019. I can tell you it has worked better for me in controlling Myeloma than any of the other treatments I have had in fighting MM since mid-2014. My Kappa and Lambda light chains have consistently remained below 1! I have Kappa Light Chain Disease and Kappa Light Chains are currently .16.

At first I received 80 mg of Selinexor weekly along with 40 mg of Dex and infusion of Kyprolis in a clinical trial administered by UCLA. That did not last long, as the Kyprolis caused a seriously diminished effective rate in the flow of blood through the left ventricle of my heart. I had to stop all treatment for a few weeks to have my heart treated with beta blocker Carvedilol. I am still taking Carvedilol, but flow rate is ok now. After a few weeks I got started on Selinexor again, but without Kyprolis. My Myeloma cells remained under good control even during the weeks I was off treatment! I started back taking 60 mg of Selinexor instead of 80 mg, and continued 40 mg of Dex which is not a problem for me. The reason we cut the dose of Selinexor was because from the beginning I had a big side effect problem of NO APPETITE! For three days after taking the Selinexor pills I would be unable to eat anything. I can tell you that situation has not changed much, even with lower dose. I take an appetite stimulator called Aprepritant for three days after taking Selinexor, but I still can't eat much but a little breakfast for three days after taking pills. What I love though is that Selinexor is simply pills I can take at home, and it is very effective. I am told my appetite problems are not common. I highly recommend Selinexor.

Let SparkCures find a Multiple Myeloma trial for you!
SparkCures.com | 888-828-2206

The Way We Were

May 2, 2020

Whelp, we have done "show us your pet," and "show us your fav car." Now how about we try, "Show us a picture of yourself from your young years, and a current picture."

I'll go first:

What About Garlic?

May 3, 2020

A friend that I respect is telling me the benefits of garlic when added to the diet. She claims garlic will improve how I feel.

Is anyone taking garlic daily as part of their journey with MM?

And so it goes, and so it goes.

Comments:

> *You may want to check out all the benefits of including garlic in your meal plan. I include it in one meal almost every day. The only thing to be aware of is that it comes from the ground and can contain bacteria, so heating it for just a few minutes or adding it to recipes is the safest way to eat it.*
>
> *Use garlic all the time in cooking. It's supposed to be good for you.*
>
> *Garlic has many wonderful properties, is natural, makes food taste better, antioxidants, etc. Read about the benefits, you'll be surprised!*

Flying Solo

May 4, 2020

Right now I'm lying in the PET scan waiting area as the IV courses through my body to settle in the trouble spots. This day I'm doing my best to make it to all my appointments alone... I'm a solo act here lately and into the future.

My dear sister Karen and I mutually agree that she simply can't handle being the primary caregiver to two very needy patients: myself and our 95 year old mother. Karen got stretched too thin. Something just had to give, and it did.

I am much more capable than mom, even though I know that as my only caregiver Karen did a LOT for me over the last seven years of my MM journey.

Today I managed to screw up a "Zoom" "telemedicine" appointment and my meds refill with that same doc.

And they told me to fast, but Karen wasn't there to say "Remember to fast for 8 hours..." So of course I forgot, and was about an inch in to a very yummy PayDay candy bar when I recalled the fasting instructions. (Note to self: eating a very sugary candy bar will seriously screw up a PET scan... "FOLLOW THE INSTRUCTIONS, NITWIT!")

So I'll drive myself home tonight.

Miss you already, Karen. Love you lots. Say "Hi" to Mom for me.

And so it goes ... and so it goes

Comments:

Losing my previously sharp mind, that could remember everything, had been hard. Developing the coping techniques that everyone else has used for years made me feel less than myself. "Self," I said, "this is not like you." And she replied, "This is You Too!" Hugs Bruce!

I set reminders and appointments on my phone. "No eating after midnight." Then I have my appointment reminder set well enough before my appointment, and I put a big note over the coffeemaker, "FASTING!" coffee is the first thing I go for in the morning.

I would surely help you if I could. Thank you Karen for all you've done.

I am praying there will be someone to help you soon. In the meantime I pray you'll be able to stay strong and confident through this ordeal.

God bless her. I have been caregiver multiple times in my family. And I think it's harder to be a caregiver than the patient.

I struggle because I don't want my daughter to go through the worst.

I've prayed to go quickly when it's time, to not linger, unable to care for myself.

I have a loving husband of 50+ years who would accompany me on any appointment. However, for the 8+ years since diagnosis, I go to all my appointments alone. It allows me to feel in control and I feel proud; I am emotionally and physically strong enough to do this alone. Time will come when I will need his help, but until then, I'm going solo.

Our caregivers are our heroes alright! Life with MM is difficult without them. Take good care of yourself because you CAN do it!

I write lots of notes. I have a pad of paper and pens on my table, and when I think of something I need I write it down. I also mark down appointments and anything I need to do.

Caregivers deserve all the credit. We're just ballast.

Bruce, remember there is Uber & Lyft... it might not be the best thing for you to be driving with your eyesight limitations at this point... some hospitals offer this free for cancer patients... talk to the Social Worker about this.

Throwing *Out* the Towel

May 4, 2020

Today was a complete screw up... end to end. I take full credit. My new middle name is "My bad."

As in Bruce "MyBad" Morgan.

Of course there's a back story... with me there always is. Readers Digest version: There once was a time when I lived most all of the time alone... just me and the dog. For decades. So let's just say a way to describe the place was "unkempt"... yeah right.

Unkempt.

Now however, as my health declines in my "late stage" part of my MM journey there's been a lot of people comment on my "unkempt" style of living.

So I hired a house cleaner, and she burns through a truck load of paper towels – just as they get next to impossible to buy in bulk because of COVID-19 shortages.

Sooooo, on his third stop this morning Mr. Bruce scores a SIX-PACK and just like THAT got the needed towels and I'm outta there.

And, you guessed it, I leave the towels in the shopping cart and drive home. I take the other groceries in... retire to my barely living living room and fall fast asleep and I emphasize FAST.

As I slept an employee of the store... a HUGE chain store... brought me the runaway six-pack of towels and set them on my front porch as I slept.

Is this a great country or what??

And so it goes and so it goes.

Comments:

> *I've done that too Bruce. I left three bags from the 99 cents store in the basket. I didn't realize until I discovered no bags in the car. I drove back to the store thinking somebody took my stuff home. I went back in the store anyways and to my surprise someone brought my bags back into the store. They were waiting for me. There are still people who believe that you should treat others as you want to be treated.* 💙 💙
>
> *Great to see that there is still honesty and good will in the world.*
>
> *Very nice people in this world.* 🤚
>
> *Things are going your way!* ❤
>
> *Uplifting. You needed that, Mr. Morton.*
>
> *There are good people everywhere!*

Selinexor

May 5, 2020

Perfect changes. That's what's in store for me, PERFECT changes. I'm really jazzed about this next leg of my MM journey.

First off, I'm out of the clinical trial for new drug Belantamab Mafodotin and the really great news is that this drug REALLY WORKS, and very soon will pass FDA guidelines and come to market to be in the arsenal our docs can use to keep us alive until a cure for MM is found

Folks, I was on this drug and it extended my life for more than six months. I am "late stage" MM, so six months is HUGE to this MM traveler.

Next up is the next PERFECT drug therapy for me. I'll be getting Selinexor, and for at least the next several months it will be my travel partner and we are going to thoroughly annoy the MM that is swimmin' 'round through my bloodstream.

After Belantamab Mafodotin, Selinexor will be my tenth line of therapy, and our hope is to get my platelet count up so I'll qualify for my next clinical trial.

Stay tuned as I get used to Selinexor and search out that next clinical trial. Yep yep, folks, I am JAZZED!

And so it goes... and so it goes.

Comments:

Best wishes. Thanks for all the updates. They help us all stay knowledgeable.

Best of luck in this game we call MM. I will be starting Selinexor within the month. Maybe we can compare notes! Good vibes from Canada coming your way.

Keep going warrior have been on the journey for 13 years not given up.

Fantastic news Bruce!!!

Many thanks for putting yourself through this trail. Your actions and determination gives us hope xXx

Good luck with Selinexor! Was not my friend!

You are blessed!

I Wanna Be Sedated

May 11, 2020

Well, I'm telling all who will listen that I'm not as sharp as I once was. The response is usually something along the lines of "It's just old age Bruce... I lose my car keys all the time..." Today's "Oops" hit me HARD, right where it really hurts.

Today I was scheduled for a bone marrow biopsy, and I showed up right on time; however, I forgot an important detail in the process. Ya, since being released from the hospital in late March I've gotten used to driving myself to my MM appointments... previously my caregiver and sister Karen drove me to ALL MM appointments... So I drove myself to my bone marrow biopsy appointment, that any common idiot knows requires a dedicated driver... because the MM patient will be too doped-up on pain killers post-procedure to drive.

So I stepped on that rake today and WHACK! Right between the eyes.

WHACK!

However, there's an easy work around: just go ahead with the BMB sans painkillers. Yep, a BMB without benefit of painkillers.

Let it be said this was worse than losing my car keys.

OUCH! Double OUCH!!

There's a lesson though I'm sure to remember next time I'm scheduled for a BMB... "Nurse, get a Band-Aid for Mr. Bruce."

And so it goes and so it goes.

Comments:

> *I have had 3 with only local anesthetic and 3 with twilight sedation. I can do it either way, but prefer the sedation.*
>
> *I've had several without pain killers! Yes, OUCH*
>
> *I've never even been offered the "doping" option. Always done just with a local at the spot. ;)*
>
> *I've done that once. Never again!*
>
> *Same here and let me tell you, that numbs the skin but NOT the area they biopsy ☺ Thankfully, it's a quick procedure and then I take 2 extra strength Tylenols... yahoo lol*
>
> *I've had 4 BMB's and not once have I even been offered anything. Wow!*

The Six-Month Gift

May 12, 2020

Well, Mr. Bruce is out of the clinical trial I've been in since November... 9x 3-week cycles... you do the math. To me those months will always represent a full half-year added to my life... Had I not answered "Yes" when I was offered the privilege of helping bringing the drug Belantamab Mafodotin to market... six months of life gifted to me, and alls I had to do was answer "Yes."

I'll now be taking a combo made up of Selinexor, Kyprolis, and Dex... and I'll be searching HARD for a next clinical trial to be in, by golly.

My first-hand experience is that clinical trials can give you extra months on this side of Glory. (And Glory will come soon enough for me, methinks.)

I'll report back to you on how this Selinexor/Kyprolis/Dexamethasone combo treats me.

Dang dang, how I hates that Dex... NASTY stuff!

And so it goes, and so it goes.

Comments:

Sorry to hear that Bruce. But glad to know that you were around longer. 😁 Pray you are able to keep kicking that can down the road.

My love is with you, and I'll carry your survival with me! Have had a week off treatment, feeling better, but no stamina or strength! Just want to sleep and can't even do that well! May all of us survivors stay banded together for enough strength to continue on! Treatment starts up again tomorrow! Joy of joys! Again!

Bruce, you are an example of a man wanting to live and also with the trials give to other people also.

Thank you Bruce for blazing a trail for us, exposing all that the journey entails, with great wit and wisdom. 💜 👊

Thanks for helping bring another drug to our arsenal 💜

On behalf of myself (caregiver), my husband (patient), and countless others fighting this disease, I THANK YOU for having the courage to trust in the unknown to help yourself and others! Continue to fight on. Be as well as you can be today, tomorrow and the many next tomorrows ahead.

Keep taking your chances until all the chances are spent!! LOVE YOU, BROTHER!!!!

Don't we all hate Dex!! Pray your meds help!

SparkCures

Let SparkCures find a Multiple Myeloma trial for you!
SparkCures.com | 888-828-2206

Sally Next Door
May 21, 2020

Well, I took my first doses of the new drugs on my tenth line of therapy: oral drug Selinexor, (Sally Next Door) and on Tuesday I got up close and medicated with old friend Kyprolis and old nemesis Dexamethasone. (Attention... personal message to Dex: I hate when I have you coursing through my body. You make life a chore, and too often you win and beat me up... but not this time. STEP ASIDE DEX, I'll beat up on YOU this time...HA!)

And so it goes and so it goes.

Comments:

I'm having the same relationship with Dex today. Grrrr.

I'm currently on Elotuzumab IV/Dex/Pomalyst and getting extremely bad Bone pain. Hoping to get off this rollercoaster and onto something that works.

I've found talking an Adavan really helps with the Dex. Dr. said it was ok.

Keep on keeping on my friend. I like the idea of telling Dex where to go!!

Life With Sally
May 22, 2020

Ok, so here's my first update on my latest line of thereby: Kyprolis and Selinexor.

Well, all was just ducky until day four when the continuous burping began, accompanied with a truly yuck taste that descended upon me.

Did I mention the "yuck" part?

Also I'm sleepy like ALL the time.

But thankfully no nausea, which was rumored to be the travel companion to the Sally Next Door.

Whelp, I'd say that, at least so far, I'm getting along just fine with my new best friend Sally. The Amazon delivery guy just tossed a six of Gatorade Zero on the front porch, and I'm hoping that tastes OK.

And so it goes, and so it goes.

Comments:

Gatorade will ADD to the belching!

We have to drink a copious amount... I drink Gatorade G2, lemon-lime. Tastes pretty good, usually drink 4 20 oz a day.

What Did You Do Today?

June 2, 2020

For the first time today I wore my new T-shirt, and it was a big hit at my Cancer Center as I lay there getting an infusion of platelets. One nurse got such a kick out of it she took a picture on her cell phone.

You all know how I preach that it's good to smile through our cancer journey, and this T-shirt produced a lot of smiles today.

I left the Cancer Center around 1:30 and on the way home I had to stop and shop for groceries. Of course I wore the same T-shirt all throughout the grocery store. It wasn't until I got home that I realized I had been wearing my "I Pooped Today" shirt all through the grocery store.

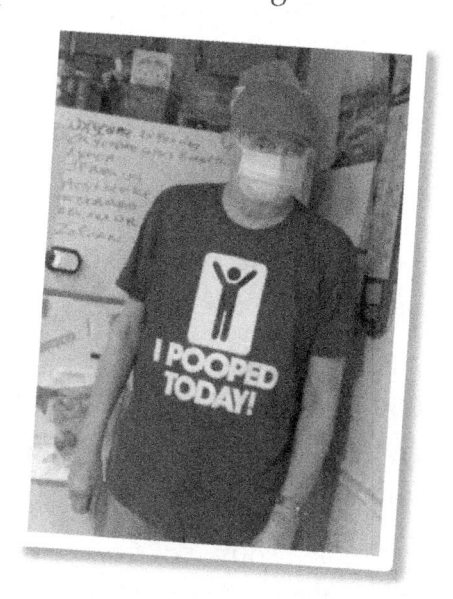

And so it goes and so it goes.

It's the Shoulder This Time
June 14, 2020

I'm still in the hospital, dagnabbit. Last Thursday the pain in my shoulder got to be too much for my oxy pain killer pills. I resorted to crying out in pain and not having a clue as to what was going on... very annoying.

Immediately upon arriving, my doc was reached and they gives me soma dat morphine and that seemed to do the trick.

From the first ER I was transferred my fav hospital; newly built, and my doc is in the same building.

Pain killers + muscle relaxers added up to be an OK pain but, whew, it hurt a lot. I slept due to the fact that all the new drugs I was given added up to quite a strong dose of sleep pills.

It took a couple of days to figure out and apply solutions: first off, I have this real major infection that we are treating with antibiotic meds.

As for the ouchy in my shoulder, they did imaging that revealed a couple of tumors that we will treat with radiation, hopefully starting tomorrow.

So perhaps I'll be sent home tomorrow... I'll see Ellie... and they decided that my infection can be put down with an ORAL pill... the alternative being in-home IV dosing of the IR. (Folks, I am VERY lousy at being my own IR infusion nurse... I've tried it and I'm very awful at it.) Once at home I may start dosing with Selinexor... or we may wait a few days.

Whew. I have a bucket FULL of new meds I'd not taken before... every color of the rainbow. Some for nausea, some for pain... some to fight infection, some for constipation... one is to chase away the shingles, some to twist at my mood.

By the time I use all my brain power remembering what the various meds are for, it's time for night-night.

And so it goes and so it goes.

Comments:

Just wondering how you were doing and sending up prayers for you. You have a wonderful mind to be able to articulate so well with all of those drugs. I hope they find help for your pain and infection!

Bruce – I don't know you yet and it doesn't matter —I am glad you shared and that's a lot to keep track of. I'm glad the unbearable pain is relieved —

You have been through the wringer once again. I love how you explain it all in happy language; that takes a real good sense of humor. ❤ *I hope you can get home to Ellie real soon and remember dogs are color blind, so she won't be much help in sorting out all those colorful pills! You're in my prayers, Bruce.* ❤

Wow, sounds like a lot! But hang in there! I hope they keep you in the hospital long enough to resolve the infection & pain. Sometimes the IV form is more effective than oral. Be sure it's for the best to switch to oral.

You have a lot going on! Do you have a med chart? I have a checklist for my meds, a.m & p.m. Also a place to note symptoms. It helps me keep track of my medicines & also when something is or isn't effective.

God bless you.

As for shingles, my oncologist has had me on Acyclovir since day one so that I would not get the shingles. Just an FYI.

Staph Meeting
June 24, 2020

Where's Bruce Morton? Well folks, my answer is a simple "I'm in the hospital."

Nothing too scary... but I am back at haunting my fav hospital that is associated with my cancer center.

This time "in" to treat a staph eppy bio infection that causes the scary infections you hear about. We are trying to tackle this infection in me at an early stage. We wasted some time going at it last week with a take-home oral antibiotic. That didn't work, soooooo... "Mr. Morgan, you've been out of the hospital for a week now and it's time to get your sorry skinny butt BACK to hospital where we can feed you lime Jell-O and treat your infection intravenously... your room on the 10th is all prepared."

So back I went to hospital with all my troubles and all my woes that I won't bore you with for fear that it would sound too much like a rant, and I don't do rants... but if'n I DID rant, I've got plenty to rant about and thank you very much, I just won't.

Like I said, I don't rant.

The short "no rant" version is that while trying to take care of this infection in me, the sonogram shows the infection has lit upon the right side of a heart valve... and is crying out to be kilt by an IV antibiotic. And yes, while going after THAT infection I had to stop taking my Selinexor.

Once the infection is cleared, "Just to be safe, Mr. Bruce, you will need 6 weeks of TWICE DAILY push (that's same as IV) of this wonder drug antibiotic."

They will let me restart Selinexor when I leave the hospital next week.

Anyhoo, I've yet to hear how I'm supposed to go about getting a twice-daily IV antibiotic into me, but that stink you smell is the idea being floated that I give myself the daily IV antibiotic. I've tried to explain that I'm not a nurse, and that I'd like to avoid being my own infusion nurse for six weeks.

So here I am... writing while dressed in a "no back" hospital gown thingy.

More news to follow

And so it goes and so it goes...

Comments:

> *Gosh darnit Bruce! I hope you sport that "no back" gown thingy up & down the halls!!! Mucho Grande love & Hugs!*

I love your posts, even though you are having so many issues. Your attitude and humor always lifts me up. Sending many prayers!! 🙏🙏🙏 ☺ ❤❤

I'm not religious, but am sending out prayers for you. ❤

Hoping you can get this under control without self-inflicted IVs. ❤

Sorry for all the mishaps... I had to do the IV at home 3 times... and I travelled too. All went well, you can do it! Home health nurse will check on you and give you instructions. Write them down... you will be a pro by the 2nd week ☺

Keep us posted 👍

Oh Bruce – tie the back of that gown!!

Wow. You sure keep your spirits up through all of this. I am not sure I could be so positive. Of course I am a wimp. Maybe they could have a Home Health Nurse come to your home to do what needs to be done. Rant as much as you want. This is the place to do it.

The Rigor and the Port
June 24, 2020

Rigor... as in "rye-gore." My current foe. Mr. Rigor has visited me twice in two days

Say hey Mr. Rigor, if you are listening in I've just one thing to say: In my best Roberto Duran voice:

"NO MAS!"

Two rounds with you is too rough on this ole bag o' bones. I've told the doc "No more visits from Mr. Rigor, and so no more Daptomycin."

Back story is that I have this really bad infection in my bloodstream, and we turned to Daptomycin to stamp it out. Wrong choice in drugs, because infused into Mr. Morgan, Daptomycin brings with it a major visit from Mr. Rigor. Twice.

There is another drug that can be substituted, so we will just switch

****

The rest of this glorious day... (Each day is a gift) I've spent waiting... and waiting... To have my Power Port removed. Senor Power Port, you see, is being blamed as the point of entry for this pesky infection I have picked up. So it's bye-bye, Senor Power Port.

Easy peasy, right? Just remove it.

Not so fast, buster. Removing the port is sorta like an operation, and that requires the patient to have at least the minimum number of platelets. Ugh. Oooops, my platelet count was too low when I got up this morning... way too low. So I've spent the day waiting as we have added bag after bag of platelets. It takes a minimum of two hours to get a bag full of platelets and infuse it into me. I've not eaten, of course, since last evening's dinner and it's 3:15p.m. So now it will end up being a full day... 24 hours... of no eating.

So I'm now waiting again, and praying that this next bag will push me above the minimum threshold of 30 that the surgeon has set and we can get on with the port removal, backed up by a sufficient number of platelets.

I'll know in an hour, I'm told, and then I just wait to get wheeled into the OR.

And so it goes and so it goes..

Comments:

That is why I don't and won't have a port. My love and prayers to you, my friend. 🤗 ❤️ 🤗

I don't have one either. I know it pisses off some nurses, but so be it.

Thoughts From a Friend

July 2, 2020

Here's a post from a FaceBook friend:

Bruce Morton UPDATE –

Hello everyone! I wanted to let everyone know I chatted with Bruce a bit tonight. He needs some extra prayers and good vibes sent his way. Bruce is battling a systematic staph infection that required him to get two hour infusions daily. If that's not bad enough, they have found two tumors on his shoulder. These will probably need radiation treatment, but that can't be done at the moment. He's not feeling to great at the moment so I am posting for him. Hopefully he will be back soon with his hilarious documentary on fighting MM.

So if you could please send an extra prayer for him tonight and Miss Ellie his faithful dog I would really appreciate it and so would Bruce. I will keep everyone posted until his return!!

Thank you!! 🖤 ☺ 🖤

Bruce Juice Is Good to Go!

July 16, 2020

Ok folks, ta-day is a celebration day. This is the story of a new MM drug that has advanced through the difficult FDA approval process.

Here are the details on the new drug PharmaLive (Belantamab Mafodotin):

> https://www.pharmalive.com/fda-panel-votes-in-favor-of-approving-gsks-multiple-myeloma-drug

You all encouraged me to be one of the 100 trial participants. I got in the trial last October, and stayed through March of this year. There were a few rough days due to side effects from the drug. In me, the drug blurred my vision to the point that I chose to stop driving, especially at night. I see fine now.

You all were counting on me, and I stayed in the trial. We even joked that Glaxo should name the new drug "Bruce Juice," but in the end the name PharmaLive won out.

And so it goes...

This is an exciting new line of treatment as a single drug, but I just betcha that there will be combos with other drugs. There will be trials to test the combos, and I encourage everyone to consider being in a future PharmaLive combo trial. The only way to give our docs new and better MM drugs is to be a clinical trial participant.

Your MM journey needs to include a clinical trial or two... or even three. Just yesterday the kind folks at SparkCures called me about a trial that might be right for me. It will be my third trial and I ask you all to please pray that the trial is right for me. I am "late stage" in my MM journey, and your encouragement and prayers are important. I need to find a trial... and quick. Yikes!

So take a moment to rest knowing that the good folks over at GlaxoSmithKline, the participating hospitals (can I put in a special Sal-Ute for my team at Siteman Cancer Center here in St. Louis... HA! WE DID IT!!!), and the hundred or more trial participants... everyone joining together to advance PharmaLive through the FDA approval process.

Hundreds of health care professionals and trial participants work each day to punch ole MM square between the eyes. Ha! Take that!

This day I sez, "Yip Yip Yahoo" and a hearty "Yabba Dabba Doo!"

And so it goes and so it goes...

Comments:

Yay!! Blessings to you Bruce Morton, always.

I would be concerned about the 27% that experience Keratopathy. That seems like a high risk depending on necessity of the treatment.

It's so good to hear from you and thank you for participating in trials, Bruce. You have advanced treatments for MM in so many ways and kept us informed, not to mention entertained! ❤

Thank you for staying in the fight for our future!

I did a trial (the Masters trial). I have my last chemo tomorrow, and they will continue to monitor me... I also encourage people to do trials.

Wow! This is great.

Awesome!

Let SparkCures find a Multiple Myeloma trial for you!
SparkCures.com | 888-828-2206

Spreading the Joy!

July 24, 2020

This is the day that the Lord hath made!

Starting out I just felt good and there are too few days when I can say that.

For my infusion all went smoothly, and there are too few days when that happens.

Then it was off to get my second haircut since the beginning of all this COVID stuff.

I chatted with the haircut girl and the subject of my cancer came up, and we chatted about that.

And at one point she remarks, "You must be a Christian…" and she smiled and I gave her a copy of my book, "Cancer Bows to a Smile."

Wow, did that make my day!

People in the service jobs meet up with all types of people, and I was reminded that it's our responsibility to demonstrate our faith with our everyday behavior.

And so it goes and so it goes.

Comments:

That was really great. Thanks for sharing.

Let us rejoice and be glad in it!

I found your book on Amazon! Ordered ☑

St. Jude Children's Research Hospital

ALSAC • Danny Thomas, Founder

Finding cures. Saving children.

Saying No to "Sally Next Door"
July 27, 2020

My treatment scheme took an important turn today. Finally in my best Nancy Reagan, I said, "No." "No" doc, I won't be taking that just now. I just said no.

Psssst... listen up for my secret of the day: It really felt good to "just say no" to a treatment line that was pert-near guaranteed to put the major upset to my tum-tum.

So I said "No;" or to be exact I said, "Wait on that" whilst I try harder to find a clinical trial that has a "Welcome Bruce" sign a-hangin' out front.

Here's the back story... Truth be told, there's no denying that my MM is rightly considered "late stage" and I'd like y'all's permission to keep on a-postin' as my condition changes... or better said, "progresses." There a reason why sometimes I don't post here. I'm still learning how to post in a lighter tone when the "news" isn't good. Leave it to me to figure that all out, and I'll keep the posts entertaining. (Insert Disney's Goofy sound effect:" Ya-Huck!!!")

Ya-Huck!!!

Ok ok... returning to the back story, the drug I did my best Roberto Duran "No Mas" on is Selinexor. I have a one cycle experience with the stuff, and it gave me uber nausea and whacked my platelet count. Ah, a whacked platelet count is the ultimate hum-dinger if you ever hope to be considered for a clinical trial.

So by refusing the Selinexor I can stay in MM feel-good land by dodging the nausea AND I protect my platelet count, which leaves it to me, my excellent MM specialist, and the good folks over at SparkCures to quickly find that trial with the "Welcome Bruce" sign.

And I need your help also to lay up a prayer... a white light of hope... double-crossed fingers... ANYTHING that might help us find that next clinical trial I'm right for. Thomas Harden, call your mother. That woman can PRAY, and it's NOW that this effort needs to be raised up.

I'm excited about what comes next. There are two trials right now that are being conducted at my Cancer Center. One might just be THE one...

Ya Huck!

And so it goes and so it goes

Comments:

Prayers being sent!!! 😷😷 What do you consider a whacked out platelet count? I have been under 50 for 7 months. I get labs almost every day, and when I am below 20, I go in for platelet transfusion at least once a week, sometimes more. Any recommendations are greatly appreciated. Healthy thoughts & healing prayers are on the way. 😷

So wonderful to see a post from you, and hope to always continue to have them coming, as long as you can do so! Please don't think your posts always need to be funny, up beat or chipper. Just be real. The real Bruce, in all the lovely, gritty or satirical, self! Sending much love and prayers, peace and healing energy!

Wonderful to receive a post from you! Please know it is not your job to entertain us! We're big girls and boys. 😛 Just know you are in our prayers and thoughts...even when you're not posting. Hoping there is a clinical trial that will be right for you. 😷😷😷

I hope you find a clinical trial that helps; as for me I stopped all treatment last summer. I am 82 and I have trouble walking. I do use the weekly pain patch for pain. So I am biding my time. Praying for you and other MM Pts.

Keep the attitude via sound effects... whatever. You are such a bright light to this page! So prayer warriors, unite and answer Bruce's request. I know I'm sending them up right now!!

Thank you for this post – I can't tell you how much it helped me. I am still in the smoldering Myeloma group, but my numbers are sneaking up. My husband and I have decided we think not to do any treatment. It sounds like the treatment is worse than the disease. I have been doing immunotherapy weekly in my home with Infusion, which seems to be helping quite a bit, but anything else seems to be something that would just ruin my life. Any comments from you would be appreciated! Thank you so much for making my morning.

Sending white light of hope & prayer your way Bruce Morton! 💖 🙏

God please continue to give Bruce & his medical team wisdom. You are a Warrior, Bruce! Praying, my friend.

Let SparkCures find a Multiple Myeloma trial for you!
SparkCures.com | 888-828-2206

All In Vein

July 28, 2020

The quip I just read on the Interweb was profound: "Don't look back... you're not headed that way."

My task for today was to do my best to get a Vancomycin infusion done without incident. Right from the start the wheels wobbled on that wagon, and I was off into the weeds.

I was just after the antibiotic infusion, but my labs showed a jump in my kidney creatinine.

Ooops... Bad sign... Stop everything... Bring out that BIG fluid bag. "Not so fast, Buster. No Vanco for you."

AND we want another blood draw, and it can't come from your port... we must have a fresh access, which means "arm draw..." and THAT means they are going to go searching for that "good vein."

The back story is that NONE of my veins are good. The last time this situation came it took a call to the phlebotomists' department to call in the best drawer in the house, but that was only after the fourth unsuccessful stab. We've all been there.

So this time I ask for the A+++ best phlebotomist in the house for the FIRST stab.

Ooops. No, BIG Ooops.

That simple request hurt the feelings of my nurse who wanted dibs on first stab.

So. Here comes A+ Phlebotomist. Tap tap. FIRST STAB and we are da-da-done, which pissed off my nurse even more. What started out as a simple infusion of Vancomycin is going to suck the life out of my entire day.

Here comes. The "F" bomb from Bruce: "Fiddlesticks!"

And so it goes and so it goes...

Comments:

Good for you! So you do have a good vein, just takes the best to find it. You have been through so much I don't think my word would be fiddlesticks.

Double fiddlesticks...

Pierre Elliot Trudeau was our Prime Minister years ago. His favorite word was "fuddleduddle". We even had mugs with that on it. Our current Prime Minister Justin Trudeau is his son.

The vein thing is a real trial! Nurses should not get their feelings hurt. They should want their patients as comfortable as possible! We are not made to be raffled off.

Aww, So sorry. I am lucky enough to have "good" veins FOR NOW! I do not have a port, so that will not last forever, I am sure. Having said that, I have had nurses MISS 3, 4 times then get another nurse WHO MISSED. Like, COME ON! (I am a nurse, give me the dang gone needle and let me draw it my darn self, at this point.) Seriously, I do not blame you for going straight to the A+ phlebotomists, I would have too. (And like I said, I have good veins.) Best of luck to you.

When you have bad veins, you have to hurt feelings sometimes! I can relate!

Oh you and your F Bomb! So happy you have your wonderful sense of humor!

Just tell your nurse you love her and smile your charming smile and I bet she'll forgive you!

She just didn't like sharing her favorite patient with others.

All is cool!

I just wish the nurses didn't take their blood draw fail so personally. They sure hate it when they have to call in the Big Guns (I prefer to call it the Big Needles) when my old veins don't cooperate.

Plotting the Course
July 31, 2020

Update on Mr. Bruce:

Yesterdee I had my first meetin'... Ugh, by phone... with my new team in the center's Palliative Care Department. I'll admit I did too much talking and not enough listening; That's because right now I feel really good... a welcome change, Ha! I will need the Palliative Care people when I feel poorly.

I'm a-thinking that this current "feel good" won't last long... (but just the same, pray that it does last a while...) and then I will be calling up my "Pal" team to choose courses of action to keep me going in comfort.

I am actively tracking down a "next" clinical trial. It is my primary goal now to engineer my counts such that I'm accepted into a next trial.

I won't have as a requirement that the trial is necessarily a right therapy to get at my personal cancer.

So... see... the way I'm figuring it, this is no longer a fight... a battle... up "against" mean ol' MM.

This is now a journey of discovery, where me and my teams focus on staying in a trial that helps bring another drug through to "FDA approved" status... a drug I can leave behind that helps everyone... like we did with Belantamab Mafodotin.

So mean ole MM, I win... you won't take life from me... my team's efforts in a trial beat you... I win. Ha!

And so it goes and so it goes

Comments:

Much love, strength and power to you Bruce! Write more later. Take care. Be safe. Be well. Remember LIVE IN TO A CURE!

I just started the BFCR4350A trial. It's supposed to be good for relapsed MM.

God bless you in your fierce dedication to our cause. Hope your "pals" are right on target!

Palliative Care is great. I hope you have a good team. Let's hope there is another clinical trial soon for you and for us. I hope you keep feeling wonderful.

Pal teams are good at any stage of this monster. Many feel it's an end stage only, but they are there to help navigate the weeds for you. They help get your message to the teams and get meds when needed. Use them. It's a great service, and they are indeed good listeners.

The Agony of da Feet

August 1, 2020

My feets.

My feets are in awful shape.

Awful.

So beware. If I talk about my feets, they are so goldarn awful I struggle to talk about them without being "gross."

Truth be told, my feets have been abused for years ... years. If I'd known I was going to live this long, I'd have taken better care of my feets.

In defense of myself, on most days I pay little attention to my feet... it's not like they ache or hurt. My feets are mostly totally numb from neuropathy.

Lucky me.

With feets that awful-looking, it's OK if they are numbed by the neuropathy.

(Ok here it comes...skip past this paragraph if you choose... I'm a-gonna tell about my awful feets: hammer toes; the toe doc and I agreed could "wait…" that was 10 years ago. I can count three toenails that have turned blue... I'll lose them but not for a while... Ugh, lemme see... yep, the feets are AWFUL.)

That brings me to today where Mr. Morgan really goofed. Ya see, right-fitting footwear can make a big difference in my overall feets' comfort throughout the day, and I just knew I was going to be on my feets a lot... a LOT... on hard concrete in my garage wrenching on my MG car. So my footwear of choice was a "flats wading boot" made for fishing sand "flats" on the sea shore.

Early in the day I tug on the flats boots and then got WAY TOO ACTIVE. Wore myself out. In Cape Girardeau speak, I got "tuckered..." PLUM tuckered.

Now comes night time, and I've retired to my barely-living living room ready for bed.

I struggle... REALLY struggle... to get the first boot off. Yep, you guessed it... me being plum tuckered, and the second must fit a LOT tighter than the first boot. For the life of me, I can't get the second boot off. I'm going off to bed. Dog Ellie watches me clump down the hall.

And so it goes and so it goes...

Comments:

> I'll tell ya, people think pedicures are a luxury; but with MM and neuropathy they are a necessity! I go every month. In between I use pure

cocoa butter on them at night, recommended by my MM specialist at DF. Gotta take care of 'em! 👣 👅

Do you have a Red Wing shoe store near you? They do a great job fitting the person to the shoe. Good quality shoes. Can you make today or tomorrow a "Bruce foot splurge day?" Shopping & a pedicure appt at a super duper safe, COVID restrictions all in place, ultimate pampering like you deserve salon?!!?!

I'm in the Dex zone tonight, struggling to get to sleep, uggh!! Earlier I forgot to add, sorry your feet are hurting so! Hoping you got the boot off, slept well & no more clumping down the hall!

I soak my feet in Johnson foot soak. I haven't found anything else that make my feet feel so good. I order it off Amazon since local stores don't carry it anymore. Try it!

Sometimes the neuropathy makes my feet feel like boulders! Fortunately that isn't a daily occurrence. Being active on my good days feels SOOOO good... but I pay for it the next day or two. Keep marching on, Bruce.

So sorry dude! Dang! Good story though. I hope you got it off! :) And that today is better for those poor feet! Soak em!

Farewell to Staph!
August 5, 2020

Got 'er dun... I'm surprised, lemme tell you.

Six weeks ago I was in the hospital and a doc introduced himself as being from infectious diseases.

"Uh oh! COVID 19?"

"Nope..."

"So what do I have, doc?"

He said that a staph infection got into me... uh huh, probably from spending so much time in germy hospitals... and the infection took up residence in one of my heart valves, a common thang in doc-speak known as endocarditis.

But there's a fix, says he: Vancomycin... massive doses of Vanco over SIX WEEKS. Yep... this doc is about to take a big chunky bite outta my summer.

Yesterday I completed dose #42. Yep, 42 IV doses over the last 42 days. Drove myself to each infusion, by golly. Gave out a lot of "Cancer Bows to a Smile" books, and met a lot of hard working infusion nurses.

But we did it, which means when I'm filling out the clinical trial applications I can proclaim that I'm infection free. Yay! Double yay! And so it goes and so it goes.

Comments:

> What a true inspiration you are to us all, Bruce! I can't get over the fact that after you have been so poorly that you actually drove yourself to the hospital. You have a fantastic team of doctors helping you... Good luck for the next part of your journey! X X

> That is tremendous news!!

> Go for a ride in the MG with Miss Ellie to celebrate!

> So thankful, 'you got 'er done!'

> Great news!! 🤗 🤗 💗

St. Jude Children's Research Hospital

ALSAC • Danny Thomas, Founder

Finding cures. Saving children.

Pump Up the Volume (2)

August 6, 2020

Finally.

I've finally started on Volume 2 of our book "Cancer Bows to a Smile."

Now remember this is *our* book, and it will include my musing about MM *and* your comments about your own MM journey. I try to post encouragements and lace in a bit of humor wherever I can.

I'll be going back through the Facebook archives to look for posts I have made over this past year.

And this past year has been full of adventure, as my own MM has progressed and now I'm living out "late stage" MM. Through my past posts I expect we will discover what it's been like for me as my MM put me in the hospital several times... a surgery on my left femur placing a titanium bar there for support after MM tumors weakened it... several other treatments came my way.

But I don't want to spoil it and tell you all about it today. This past year, with MM as my constant travel companion, and with the support of everyone here on Facebook, it has been a marvelous journey, indeed.

There's a lot for my editor Gryf Ketcherside and me to sift through, but it feels good to say, "The work on book 2 has begun!"

And so it goes and so it goes.

Comments:

I find your posts candid, real, uplifting, hopeful, and humorous. This MM is a crazy roller coaster. I thought I was in the clear after my 1st transplant, not so much. Had high hopes for CAR-T, again, wasn't in the cards. As we all know... there is no rhyme or reason. I am with you on constant companion. I am at the doctors with chemo, transfusions, labs, shots, radiation, at least 5 days a week. Takes a beating on my mind and body. So.... from the bottom of my heart, thank you for being there to lift me up out and get outta the dark places. ☺ 🙏 ☺

Bruce I have learned in the last couple of years that a big ol' smile is coming up when I see your name at the top of a post! You never disappoint.

It has been great seeing genuine friendships develop from others like yours and Thomas' and yours and Megan's. Lifting one another is heartfelt, and encouraging of itself. Please know we are always here if you need us. Remember we need to hear from you or we get concerned. Have a good day, friend.

Bruce - can't wait for volume 2... Volume 1 was wonderful. You have such a unique way of dealing with MM, and we all need to find our own ways to deal with it. I personally deal with it much like you....straight forward and with humor, but...I cannot compare myself to you...you have mastered it to a "T". Your MM warriors are here for you and look forward to your posts and your new book. ❤🙈❤🙈

Awesome! Can't wait for #2!!! LOL... you call MM your constant travel companion... I call my MM & Scleroderma my "Roommates," and I try to keep them stuffed in the closet so they don't act up! LOL

I'm so happy for you to be feeling well enough to do this!!! Can't wait to get book 2!

Looking forward to it being finished!

We're Doing Number 2 ☺

August 23, 2020

Well folks, work on Volume 2 of our book is coming along nicely. Yippee! With the help of our editor we've completed 125 pages.

Good stuff.

For those of you that are new here, about a year ago I completed work on a book that chronicles my journey with MM. I post rather frequently here, and when I do y'all add your comments. That's why I refer to this second book also as OUR book.

Anyone that is on their own MM journey and deals with MM daily, when you comment on my posts, you become part of our book(s). It's important to me to always clarify: although I'm listed as the author, the book(s) are OUR book(s).

You can find Volume 1 by searching "Cancer Bows to a Smile" by Bruce Morton on Amazon.

And so it goes and so it goes.

Comments:

Thank you for posting this. I'll go to Amazon & order it today!!

Love this!

I am new here, having been diagnosed July 15. I am like a babe in the woods, trying to get up to speed with words and abbreviations of words that I've never heard in my life. I start the drugs on Tuesday. Fingers and toes crossed for an uneventful drug therapy.

I have the first book. Wonderful book. Highly recommend.

I just bought "Cancer Bows to a Smile" Volume 1 – can't wait to read it.

Perhaps a top-down ride on a country road in the MG with Miss Ellie as a deserving break!

I can't wait until Volume 2 is finished.

SparkCures

Let SparkCures find a Multiple Myeloma trial for you!
SparkCures.com | 888-828-2206

The Road Ahead

August 23, 2020

My MM doc is now, thankfully, being frank with me about the condition of my condition.

My MM specialist is a fabulous doc; however, it was always his style to never venture too far out into the future when commenting about my MM. I heard a lot of, "We'll cross that bridge..." talk.

But now I'm in a much later stage of MM, and "We'll cross that bridge..." wasn't cutting it. So a few weeks ago I pressed him for more... more about my condition. This week I was sorta stunned by what I heard from him.

Yeah... stunned.

Ka-bong*

Ya see, I was pressing him to get me into another clinical trial. Being accepted into another trial became my focus in life.

However, in the doc's view of my condition I'll never qualify for another trial. The MM, along with seven and a half years of treatment, has whacked my bone marrow to such an extent that I'll never have enough blood platelets to qualify.

I feel like I'm letting you all down. I know in my heart though that I gave it my best.

So, my journey with MM takes a turn. We have a plan that will not include any trials.

I like the new plan. The first phase is to lay off all treatment of the MM. I'm feeling great... yes, GREAT for a change. The MM is kinda coming back, but it's not raging back... and until I have to, I want to go through this journey sans treatment.

After that, there are a few treatments that may be left for me. "We'll cross that bridge..."

And so it goes and so it goes.

*Who among us can recall the origins of the El-Kabong? Well, circa 1959 we tuned in to the Hanna-Barbera cartoons on Saturday mornings, and there was a character named Quick Draw McGraw; his sidekick was Baba Looey, and his alter ego was "El Kabong," who would lay out his foes by bonging them on the head with his guitar.

Comments:

Bruce, you will always be a hero, at least to me. Thank you for all the trials you've bravely gone through to hopefully help other MM warriors. You deserve a break (not talking about them bones, either!) Relax and have some fun for a while!

Please keep us updated with your antics, my friend. Keep on fighting, sending you lots of hugs and prayers.

You are a BRAVE MM Fighter and that doesn't stand for Mixed Martial Arts! You have helped so many, and will continue to help long after this. Thank you for your frankness and willingness to be that voice for so many of us in our differing stages.

Thank you for your friendship as well, and I so pray that we will one day be able to see each other again soon without all this "6 feet apart, don't touch him, now go wash your hands!!!" ☺ Stay encouraged and know we are all here to cheer you on!!!

You can never let us down. You are more than platelets and MM.

Your joy, humor, honesty and zest for life carries us. KNOW YOU MATTER MORE than anything.

LOVE YOU Bruce Morton!

Bruce. Live the moment. I know you've heard that many times. If it's any comfort, just know I'm right behind ya. In fact we all are, like it or not. By the way, it's Baba bouey (Howard Stern reference). Cheers.

That little Baba Looey burro was so cute. They were still airing that funny little cartoon in the late 60's when I would watch with my 5 big brothers... then we'd "kabong" each other the rest of the day!

You have done your clinical trial part. Enjoy feeling good for a change!

Bruce – thanks for providing the update. YOU have the attitude to "bounce" back... maybe not as "high" as you wanted. Your attitude will carry you through. And you are not letting us down. You may not be able to hear it, but your warriors are cheering for you! Hopefully, you can stay off meds so that you can feel good for a while. We are here for you!!

Very glad that you are feeling great, Bruce. You deserve it... All the best of luck with the (very slow) progress of your progression.

Hey, we're still in this together! TOGETHER.

Enjoy life the best you can, as you always have. You continue to help many with your spirit, humor and fight. I pray blessings over your life.

Thank you for all the trials you've participated in. You probably don't know how many of us you have helped, and will help! Now it's time to enjoy the relief of no treatments for as long as you can.

Runaway Wheelchair!

August 25, 2020

I live on a hill.

And living on a hill, I suppose I should know better... but not today.

Today I was reminded once again that in the thinking department my brain is significantly compromised.

I mean I live on a hill... I should have known... right?

This adventure started when I decided to work on my priceless little British sports car. The fact that at 8.9 hemoglobin count I'm too weak to get out of the driver's seat just means that I need a lot of help if I decide to go for a drive.

So to get into my crowded garage, I move a small amount of accumulated junk just to get to the MG car: lawn chair, trash cans, TWO wheelchairs, and a folded up walker get pushed out onto the driveway.

The sloped driveway. (Ok, so the driveway slopes... I should have known better, right?)

I should have known that it's important to secure your wheelchairs if your driveway is sloped and you live on a hill.

Yep. The newest wheelchair... and it's full of garage junk... car wash bucket... mini vac... the newest, and as it turns out, best rolling wheelchair is ga-ga-gone when it comes time to re-stuff the garage with stuff.

I figure to find the runaway chair crashed at the end of the driveway which... did I mention it's sloped?

But no. This wheelchair takes a run down the sloped drive and it musta shot down the middle of the street.

It was packed with garage crap so as I went to retrieve the runaway chair, I made sure I retrieved all my good garage stuff.

I'm bare foot.

Since the neuropath has total numbed my feet I didn't figure that it would matter to chase after the chair barefoot down the neighborhood street.

I was wrong.

Apparently the wheelchair picked up a *lot* of speed zooming past four houses down to the house at the end of the cul-de-sac. It picked up enough speed to mow down some previously nice looking azaleas...

Alls I wanted to do is get my chair and hobble home.

But no.

One last obstacle.

The wheelchair was deep into the neighbors flower bed, and I could juuuuuust reach it if I planted juuuust one of my now throbbing numb feet into the flower bed filled with... Oh no!

Lava rock!

Ouch. Double ouch!

But I pile all my garage crap back into my shiny new runaway wheelchair and head up the hill to home where I'll enjoy an ice cold Special K protein drink as I soak my feet in Epsom Salts.

And so it goes and so it goes.

Cancer Bows to a Smile, Volume 2

Acknowledgements

By Grant Adkisson, Pastor
Cañon City Colorado Cowboy Church

What kind of man is diagnosed with severe cancer with only a short time to live and writes a book about what he is experiencing to encourage other people?

That man is Bruce Morton.

But stop right there... hold on... before you give him any praise!

Before you give him any credit... before you begin to think he's super human... I need to tell you his secret! (Just make sure that you don't let him know I told you.)

The way all of those things have been done by Bruce Morton is because HE CHEATS!

No question about it!

How does he cheat? He doesn't do all those things by himself!

And don't try to figure out who the other person is that helps him, because it's not a person on Earth.

The way Bruce cheats in doing all these things that are not normal, not even possible humanly speaking, is because he has let God do it all through him!

Jesus Christ lives right in the middle of his body! Jesus Christ has indwelt his body and mind and his life!

Now you might be thinking "isn't that true for many people? Possibly even you yourself. Yes it is, but many Christians don't really "let God do it."

They don't depend on Almighty God to live through their lives on a daily basis, and they try instead to go through life depending on their own strength.

A statement that I have made thousands of times across the United States and around the world is this: "God, I can't... you never said I could. You can, and you promised that you would." That describes how Bruce Morton "cheated!"

No wonder there are so many supernatural things evident in and through his life. It is Almighty God doing it through him... which is actually the simple key to the victorious Christian life for every believer.

This could be illustrated by the story of a young boy that just got home from Sunday school and when asked by his father how his class was, he answered that he didn't like it because the story from the Bible couldn't be true. He went on to say the class was about Jonah being swallowed by a fish... living in its stomach and then being spit out on the seashore to do a mission trip... the boy just didn't believe it.

His dad then said, "If God is big enough to make this whole world, don't you think he could make a fish big enough to swallow a person?" The little boy said "well if you are going to bring God into the story, that changes everything. With God anything is possible!"

Now that's just how you are reading this book in your hand. Through Bruce's life and through your life and mine when we bring God in to each part of it, ANYTHING is possible.

Grant

I asked Grant Adkisson to write up that acknowledgment to this Volume 2 in our series of "Cancer Bows to a Smile" books. His words are "spot on." Yes, all the credit goes to God. The more I learned to set my sights on God's plan for my life... particularly my life after being diagnosed with multiple myeloma in 2013... I've discovered how wonderful God's perfect plan for my life truly is every day of the MM journey.

I trust that you will enjoy this Volume 2, and I've already started on Volume 3. Alas, there most likely won't be a Volume 4. As my MM journey nears a close, I am comforted in the arms of Almighty God.

For those who would like to know "What denomination are you?" it's certainly fine just to ask or better yet, lemme tell ya. In recent years I've come to follow Pastor Andrew Farley and the online streaming versions of "Church Without Religion." They're based in Lubbock, Texas with "followers" like myself worldwide. The primer of this New Covenant ministry is "The Naked Gospel," authored by Pastor Farley and available on Amazon.

> "Man-made religion tells us that we're at the heart of the equation. We must 'do.' And we're never done

until we hit heaven and find out if it was enough. In contrast, the New Covenant is all about what Jesus has done to provide an unbreakable connection with God and guaranteed growth in Him."

Andrew Farley

If you would like to learn more about this ministry, visit churchwithoutreligion.com.

Bruce

Glossary and Abbreviations

MM: Multiple Myeloma

BMB: Bone Marrow Biopsy

LP: Lumbar Puncture test

SCT: Stem Cell Transplant procedure

CAR-T: A new and promising treatment for MM... Google it

DEX: Dexamethasone steroid, given as an injection or orally

Please Donate to St. Jude Children's Research Hospital

For many years, my charity of choice has been St. Jude Children's Research Hospital.

St. Jude Children's Research Hospital
ALSAC • Danny Thomas, Founder
Finding cures. Saving children.

St. Jude's is doing fabulous work... saving kids' lives. They are wonderful stewards of the money that is donated to them. Please go to stjude.org and give $20 or more if you can. Hey, no kid should have to struggle with cancer, and no young family should be burdened having to pay for cancer care.

Thanks!

Made in the USA
Monee, IL
17 September 2022